VOLUME 7

Minnesota Monographs in the Humanities

Leonard Unger, editor

A History of
the Alans in the West

*From Their First Appearance
in the Sources of Classical Antiquity
through the Early Middle Ages*

BERNARD S. BACHRACH

UNIVERSITY OF MINNESOTA PRESS
Minneapolis

Library of Congress Catalog Card Number: 73-77710

ISBN 0-8166-0678-1

For DEBBY

Preface

In 1922 the Russian scholar M. I. Rostovtzeff wrote, "In most of the work on the period of migrations, the part played by the Sarmatians and especially by the Alans in the conquest of Europe is almost ignored. But we must never forget that the Alans long resided in Gaul, . . . that they invaded Italy, and that they came with the Vandals to Spain and conquered Africa. . . ." In 1963 George Vernadsky echoed Rostovtzeff's remarks and concluded that during the intervening four decades still no major historical investigation of the Alans in the West had appeared.[1] The present study is aimed at filling this lacuna in the history of early medieval Europe which has already existed too long.[2]

1. M. I. Rostovtzeff, *Iranians and Greeks in South Russia* (Oxford, 1922), p. 237. George Vernadsky, "Eurasian Nomads and Their Impact on Medieval Europe," *Studi Medievali*, 3rd ser., IV (1963), 421. Vernadsky has made numerous contributions to the study of the Alans, which are synthesized in the article mentioned above. For Vernadsky's complete bibliography on the Alans and related subjects through 1963, see *Essays in Russian History: A Collection Dedicated to George Vernadsky*, ed. Alan D. Ferguson and Alfred Levin (Hamden, Conn., 1964), pp. xiii–xxv.

2. The most recent surveys of the Alans are R. Wenskus, "Alanen," *Reallexikon der germanischen Altertumskunde*, I.2 (Berlin, 1970), 122–124; J. Ozols, "Alanen," *ibid.*, pp. 124–126. Ozols discusses the archaeological materials and this discussion is supplemented by T. Sulimirski, *The Sarmatians* (New York, 1970). Wenskus's attempt to cover Alan history in less than three pages falls short of W. Tomaschek, "Alanen," *RE*, I, cols. 1282–1285. Sulimirski's treatment of the Alans in the West is less than four pages long (pp. 185–188). See my review of this work in *AHR*, LXXVI (1971), 1525–1526. In none of these works noted above are the latest studies of the

vii

A HISTORY OF THE ALANS

A history of the Alans in the West during the *Völkerwanderung* and the early Middle Ages, like histories of the other peoples during those hectic times, helps us to obtain a better understanding of the end of the ancient world and the beginning of the Middle Ages. Unlike the various German tribes which dominated the migrations numerically and have dominated the historical literature of the migrations ever since, the Alans were Indo-Iranian nomads. In fact, the Alans were the only non-Germanic people of the migration period to make important settlements in Western Europe. The Huns were driven out of Europe; the Avars, Magyars, Bulgars, and Slavs confined their settlements to Eastern Europe. As a unique phenomenon in the history of Western Europe, the Alans have long deserved to be studied.

The history of this nomadic people begins in the West not when they first entered the Roman empire but when Westerners first became aware of the Alans and left some written record of their observations. Therefore, to provide for a better understanding of the Alans' migration westward and their reception, the first chapter of this monograph is devoted primarily to what Westerners thought and said about the Alans before the *Völkerwanderung*. Secondly, an attempt has been made to ascertain the nature of Alan culture in the period before migration. This latter task is far more difficult than the former because frequently we cannot accept the information provided in the written sources at its face value. In addition, the archaeological evidence is often ambiguous, and we cannot, for example, determine precisely whether a burial or an artifact is Alan, Sarmatian, or Roxolan.[3]

Alans in the West consulted. An incomplete collection of texts of the classical and Byzantine periods in which the Alans are mentioned is to be found in Iu. Kulakovsky, *Alany po svedeniiam klassicheskikh i vizantiiskikh pisatelei* (Kiev, 1899).

3. The virtually insurmountable problems of gaining exact knowledge of the history of nomad culture from archaeological evidence are set out in a most convincing fashion by E. A. Thompson, *A History of Attila and the Huns* (Oxford, 1948), pp. 4–5. Joachim Werner, *Beiträge zur Archäologie des Attila-Reiches* (Munich, 1956), illustrates even in the choice of his title the great difficulties attendant upon ascribing particular styles or objects to particular groups, especially when these groups are nomadic. On the problem of drawing specific conclusions about a particular people from archaeo-

PREFACE

As the foregoing remarks imply, the Alans left us no corpus of written materials for the period under discussion; like most nomads of the ancient and medieval world they were nonliterate. It was only after the Alans were assimilated into the late Roman-early medieval world that some of them attained literacy, and then only in Latin. Much of the extant information about the Alans is provided by certain contemporary and near contemporary individuals whose interests were more often than not focused on a subject other than the Alans. Therefore, information about the Alans survives in some unlikely sources, and only by critically examining this written evidence can we hope to understand a people whose culture and history largely remains obscure to modern scholars.

A historical inquiry such as this one necessarily evokes the question of who exactly is being studied. In dealing with this problem, I have employed what may be called a modified nominalist approach. If the sources use the Latin term *Alani* (Gr. 'Αλανοί), I have assumed that the information is relevant to my study. Conversely, if other barbarian groups such as the Roxolani or Aorsi, who were also Indo-Iranian nomads, appear in the sources but the Alans are not specifically mentioned, I have judged that the information is not relevant to my inquiry. This method has been modified in two cases. In the first, a writer might mention the *Alani* but mean some other group with a similar name such as the Celtic *Alauni*. The contrapositive of this case has also arisen. In the second, the source might mention the Roxolani or some other Indo-Iranian group but have confused them with the *Alani* because of similar customs or linguistic pat-

logical evidence without the support of written evidence, see the brief remarks in my review of Sulimirski's book, *AHR*, pp. 1525–1526. On the general problem of using archaeological evidence for writing history, see Thomas F. O'Rahilly, *Early Irish History and Mythology* (Dublin, 1946), p. 440, and P. H. Sawyer, *The Age of the Vikings* (London, 1962), pp. 48–50. For a highly critical attack on the intellectual validity of identifying certain styles or traditions with particular ethnic or "racial" groupings, see B. H. Slicher van Bath, "Dutch Tribal Problems," *Speculum*, XXIX (1949), 319–338. Slicher van Bath maintains that during periods when many peoples are in movement and there is a considerable degree of interaction between them it is preferable to emphasize the mélange nature of artifacts.

terns. Thus, where the nominal method led to a dubious result, I went beyond it, adopting a more flexible approach.[4] The problems raised by the nominal method obtain largely in chapter I, which deals with the Alans when they were beyond the borders of the empire and when information concerning them was fragmentary and sometimes unreliable. After the migrations and during the early Middle Ages, the Alans who had come west and their descendants were generally known to those who commented on their activities. From this point onward there is very little terminological confusion.

Bernard S. Bachrach

4. See ch. I, n. 19, and appendix II.

Acknowledgments

During the seven years that I worked on the Alans, I have incurred many debts to friends, colleagues, and institutions. I owe special thanks to the late Otto Maenchen-Helfen who encouraged my study of the Alans and gave generously of his time long after he had retired as a professor at the University of California, Berkeley. Richard W. Emery, professor emeritus at Queens College, C.U.N.Y., gave me invaluable help with southern French sources. Professor Frank Clover of the University of Wisconsin and Tom B. Jones, regents professor of history at the University of Minnesota, read the entire manuscript at one or another stage in its preparation and made many useful and challenging suggestions. My colleagues Professor F. R. P. Akehurst of the French Department at Minnesota provided some important philological observations and Professor Tom Noonan of the History Department kept me informed of Russian scholarship. It would not have been possible for me to have written this monograph had not Mrs. Gertrude Battel and her staff of the Inter-Library Loan Division of Wilson Library, University of Minnesota, been so cooperative and efficient in securing so many obscure and rare publications. I am also grateful to the American Council of Learned Societies, the Graduate School of the University of Minnesota, and the Office of International Programs at Minnesota, all of whom provided grants that helped make possible my research and writing. My wife, Debby, to whom this book is dedicated once again took time from her own scholarly work to help with the proofreading and the index.

Contents

CONTENTS *Continued*

Abbreviations

AHR	*American Historical Review*
BEHE	*Bibliothèque de l'Ecole des Hautes Etudes*
CAH	*Cambridge Ancient History*
CIL	*Corpus Inscriptionum Latinarum*
CSEL	*Corpus Scriptorum Ecclesiasticorum Latinorum*
EHR	*English Historical Review*
FHG	*Fragmenta Historicorum Graecorum*
HA	*Scriptores Historiae Augustae*
HGL	*Histoire General de Languedoc*
JRS	*Journal of Roman Studies*
MGH	*Monumenta Germaniae Historica*
AA	*Auctores Antiquissimi*
LL	*Leges*
SSRG ius	*Scriptores Rerum Germanicarum in Usum Scholarum*
SSRG n.s.	*Scriptores Rerum Germanicarum, new series*
SSRL	*Scriptores Rerum Langobardicarum et Italicarum*
SSRM	*Scriptores Rerum Merovingicarum*
PLM	*Poetae Latini Minores*
RBPH	*Revue Belge de Philologie et d'Histoire*
RE	Pauly-Wissowa (-Kroll), *Real-Encyclopädie der classischen Altertumswissenschaft*
RH	*Revue Historique*

A History of the Alans in the West:
From Their First Appearance in the Sources of Classical
Antiquity through the Early Middle Ages

CHAPTER I

Alans beyond the Frontier

THE EARLIEST known mention of the Alans in the West appears in Seneca's *Thyestes*, a play which was probably written during the fourth decade of the first century A.D. or perhaps a little earlier. Seneca has a messenger ask, "What region is this? Is it Argos? Is it Sparta . . . ? Is it Corinth . . . ? Is it the Danube which gives to the fierce Alans (*feris Alanis*) the chance to escape? Is this the Hercanian land buried beneath its eternal snows or that of the nomad Scythians?"[1]

Argos, Sparta, Corinth, the Danube, the Hercanian land, and the Scythians were all recognizable to Roman audiences; only the Alans appear in no earlier surviving source. The messenger's remarks, however, give no indication that Seneca wanted to draw his listener's attention to the Alans in this context. In this passage the Alans serve no dramatic purpose which distinguishes them from the other people and places in the list nor are they mentioned again throughout the play. Therefore, it seems likely that Seneca's contemporaries were sufficiently aware of the Alans so that they would not be distracted by hearing their name in a list of commonplaces.

1. Seneca, *Thyestes*, ll. 627ff. E. Täubler, "Zur Geschichte der Alanen," *Klio*, IX (1909), 14, 15, 17, n. 5, suggests that Seneca may have meant the Don and not the Danube. The text, however, clearly indicates Hister (Danube). Cf. Rostovtzeff, *Iranians and Greeks*, p. 116, and J. G. C. Anderson, "The Eastern Frontier from Tiberius to Nero," *CAH*, X (1934), 777.

Seneca's remarks do, however, suggest that Alans from north of the Danube were raiding south across the river into Roman territory and then escaping back across the river where the soldiers of Rome did not or could not pursue them. This kind of activity might well have been the reason why the Alans became known at Rome in such a relatively short time.

The Alans next appear in Lucan's *Civil Wars,* an epic poem written in the early sixties of the first century A.D., which dealt with the wars between Pompey and Caesar that had taken place more than a century earlier. Though the poem has a certain historical flavor, Lucan was not averse to introducing imaginative elements. While discussing Pompey's plans after the battle of Pharsalia, Lucan notes that the defeated general arranged with a certain Deiotarus, his loyal follower and a king of Galatia, to raise the Eastern peoples against Caesar. At this point Pompey indicates that his past exploits in the East had led him to march through the Caspian Gates against the "tough and always warring Alans" (*duros aeterni Martis Alanos*), though their neighbors, the Parthians, he left in peace.[2]

There is no reason to believe that Pompey ever fought against the Alans or that he pursued them through the Caspian Gates. Yet the connection of the Alans with the area of the Caspian Gates and as neighbors of the Parthians was intended to lend a realistic note to Lucan's narrative and thus would probably not have seemed out of place to his audience.[3]

In another part of the *Civil Wars,* Lucan, discussing the ambiguous nature of Caesar's bravery, mentions three militarily imposing peoples who would normally frighten the average man but whom Caesar did not fear. Lucan writes, "Neither the Alans or the Scythians, or the Moors, who attack the enemy with spears could harm him."[4]

From both Seneca and Lucan it seems clear that their audi-

2. Lucan, *De Bell. Civ.,* VIII, ll. 215ff. See also Täubler, "Alanen," pp. 14, 17.
3. E. M. Sanford, "Nero and the East," *Harvard Studies in Classical Philology,* XLVIII (1937), 98.
4. Lucan, *De Bell. Civ.,* X, ll. 454ff. Cf. Täubler, "Alanen," p. 14, n. 4.

ences were aware of the prowess of the Alan fighting men. These audiences presumably knew enough about the Alans so that literary allusions to them could be made. It is only from Josephus, however, that we obtain some more definite idea of when and how knowledge of the Alans reached the West. In his *Jewish Antiquities,* written toward the end of the first century, Josephus notes that the Roman Emperor Tiberius, probably in A.D. 35 (the time of the writing of Seneca's *Thyestes*), made an effort to obtain the aid of the Iberians and the Albanians against the Parthians. Though neither of these groups lent direct military aid to Rome at this time, Josephus recounts that they did permit the Alans to pass freely through their lands and the Caspian Gates as well so that they might fight against the Parthians as allies of Rome. This the Alans did, and, according to Josephus, they did it very well.[5]

In his *Jewish Wars,* written during the seventies of the first century, Josephus provides additional information on the Alans. He states that the Alans are a "Scythian people" who inhabit the area along the banks of the river Don and the Sea of Azov. Of perhaps equal importance is his observation that he had dealt with these matters somewhere before. This previous mention does not survive, but it does indicate that there was additional information available in the West about the Alans toward the middle of the first century A.D., if not earlier.[6]

After providing this geographic and ethnographic information, Josephus describes what seems to have been a rather recent Alan raid in force into Media and beyond in which the Alans harassed the Parthians and took large amounts of booty, including ransom for important personages whom they had captured. The Alans took those captives who were not ransomed back with them to their own lands. Josephus notes, too, that opposition by the peoples who were attacked made the Alans more savage than usu-

5. Josephus, *Ant. Jud.,* XVIII, 4, 96ff. Cf. Rostovtzeff, *Iranians and Greeks,* p. 116, and Täubler, "Alanen," pp. 15–16.
6. Josephus, *De Bell. Jud.,* VII, 4, 244ff. See Karl Müllenhoff, *Deutsche Altertumskunde,* II (Berlin, 1892), 42; Täubler, "Alanen," p. 15, especially n. 2; and Anderson, "Eastern Frontier," p. 777, n. 3, n. 4.

al. He also points out that the lasso was one of their weapons.[7]

It was this raid which probably inspired the Parthian King Vologasus I to request Roman aid against the Alans. Vologasus asked Vespasian to ally with him against the Alans and specifically requested that one of the emperor's sons lead the Roman army. Domitian, who was eager to undertake the campaign, did not manage to get it underway, however, and no expedition against the Alans was launched.[8]

Josephus's account of Alan activities against the Parthians is given some support by Suetonius's *Life of Domitian*, and his remarks on the Alans' ethnic background are buttressed by the observations of his contemporary, the elder Pliny. In his chapter on Dacia and Sarmatia in the *Natural History*, Pliny comments, "From this place [the mouth of the Danube], all the peoples are indeed Scythian, though various others have occupied the bordering shores; in one place the Getae, whom the Romans call Daci; in another the Sarmatians, whom the Greeks call Sauromatians, and a group of these called the Hamaxobii or the Aorsi; there are also others who are of Scythian origin and of servile origin and also the Trogodytae; and nearby the Alans and the Roxolans. In the higher places, moreover, between the Danube and the Hercynian forest and as far as the Pannonian winter quarters at Carnuntum and the borders of the Germans, dwell the Sarmatian Iazyges."[9]

During the period from the reign of Tiberius to that of Vespasian, Western interest in the Alans was stimulated primarily by their position as an imperial ally. The Alans' effectiveness against the Parthians helped them to gain a substantial military reputation in the West while at the same time making the Parthians less bellicose toward Rome. The Alans who supported

---

7. Josephus, *De Bell. Jud.*, VII, 4, 248ff. Täubler, "Alanen," p. 18. N. Debevoise, *A Political History of Parthia* (Chicago, 1938), p. 200, points out that the date has been placed ca. A.D. 72. See the bibliography he cites in n. 55.

8. Suetonius, *V. Domit.*, 2.2. Debevoise, *Parthia*, p. 200.

9. Pliny, *Nat. Hist.*, IV, 12, 25ff. George Rawlinson, *The Sixth Great Oriental Monarchy* (New York, 1872), p. 291, n. 2; Täubler, "Alanen," p. 26, n. 2; and Müllenhoff, *Deutsche Altertumskunde*, III, 53.

Rome against the Parthians south of the Caspian Sea were, however, but one of several Alan groups of which Westerners had knowledge. Some Alans dwelt north of the Danube and may even have raided across the river into imperial territory. Other Alan groups lived along the shores of the Black Sea and the Sea of Azov and along the banks of the river Don in close proximity to several other Sarmatian peoples as well as among some Germanic peoples.

Through the end of the first century, literary men continued to refer to the Alans. Valerius Flaccus mentions them in his epic poem *The Argonautica*. He locates them in the Crimean area and has them taking part in Pontic politics. On one occasion Valerius calls them "fiery" (*ardentes*) and at another point he describes them as "wretched" (*miser*) — perhaps alluding to the mean material level of nomadic life.[10]

The satirist Martial mentions the Alans in a poem to a lady of uncertain virtue named Caelia. He writes, "Caelia you give yourself to Parthians, you give yourself to Germans, you give yourself to Dacians. You do not reject the beds of Cilicians and Cappadocians. From the Pharian city the Egyptian stud comes for you as does the black Indian from the Red Sea. You don't even draw the line at the circumcised members of the Jewish race and the Alan with his Sarmatian mount does not pass you by. What is your reason that although you are a Roman girl you do not find pleasure in the members of the Roman race?"[11]

Martial's list of Caelia's favorites includes a cross section of barbarians and Easterners who in general were well known to the Roman people and who probably seemed both exotic and inferior to the Roman listener. Martial's mention of the Alan with his Sarmatian horse may be seen as a specific though poetic reference connecting these two Asiatic peoples. Pliny had earlier

10. Valerius Flaccus, *Argonautica,* VI, ll. 42ff. Müllenhoff, *Deutsche Altertumskunde,* III, 78, and Täubler, "Alanen," p. 15. It is worth quoting here the observation on Valerius Flaccus by Debevoise (*Parthia,* p. 202): "The work of Valerius Flaccus, a part of which must have been composed about this time, clearly mirrors Roman interest in the Alani and in the Caucasus region."
11. Martial, VII, 30. Cf. Täubler, "Alanen," pp. 27–28.

talked of both Sarmatians and Alans as Scythians, and Josephus explicitly considered the Alans to have been Scythians. Although Westerners seem not to have had substantial everyday contact with the Alans, Martial's remarks suggest that some of them, perhaps in the entourage of an Eastern prince, may have visited Rome, and thus the xenophile Caelia may indeed have had the opportunity to learn of the Alans' exotic mount.

Though Tacitus apparently ignored the Alans, they were noticed by his contemporaries and near contemporaries.[12] The Alan raids into the Parthian kingdom which had aided Rome's Eastern policy under Tiberius and Vespasian were extended into Armenia and Cappadocia during Hadrian's reign. Armenia, however, was a Roman satellite and Cappadocia was an imperial province. In the latter area, Flavius Arrianus, Hadrian's legate, engaged the Alans in battle and drove them out of Roman territory.[13]

Arrian was the first Western general, whom we know to have faced the Alans in combat and he drew up battle plans to deal with them. A part of this work, *Contra Alanos*, survives, and along with another of Arrian's works, *The Tactica*, it provides some very useful information. The Alans and the Sarmatians, according to Arrian, are mounted spearmen who charge the enemy forcefully and rapidly. Arrian points out that an infantry phalanx supported by the use of missiles is the most effective way to stop an Alan attack. When the Alans are inundated by a shower of missiles and find that they cannot shatter the infantry phalanx with their charge, they can be expected to retreat. Arrian sees this as a crucial point in the battle because the Alans have the capacity to turn such a retreat into victory. Apparently the Alans used a tactic that has come to be called a "feigned retreat"; if the infantry which had previously faced them broke ranks and followed the fleeing enemy, the latter would turn their horses and attack the footmen who had lost formation during the pursuit. It is indicated in later sources that the feigned retreat had

12. On Tacitus, see appendix I.
13. Dio Cassius, LXIX, 15. Täubler, "Alanen," p. 26; M. I. Rostovtzeff, "The Sarmatae and Parthians," *CAH*, XI (1936), 111; Mommsen, *Röm. Gesch.*, V, 405; and Sanford, "Nero and the East," p. 98, n. 2.

been a well-developed steppe cavalry tactic used not only by the Alans but by the Huns, Magyars, and Turks as well. Besides the feigned retreat which was used to provoke the precipitous disintegration of an enemy infantry phalanx, the Alans also deployed against the enemy flank using a maneuver that appeared to be a headlong retreat. Thus, while the enemy's infantrymen were concentrating upon the Alans retreating in front of them, the Alans' horsemen would suddenly wheel and attack on the flank.[14]

Arrian sought to prevent the success of the feigned retreat by sending part of his cavalry in hot pursuit of the enemy and by keeping the other horsemen in ranks and moving them at a slower pace. The infantry was under standing orders not to break its phalanx formation regardless of how disorganized the enemy cavalry appeared to be; it was to march forward slowly to support its own cavalry. Arrian had his infantry defend against the Alans' flanking movements by hurling his cavalry at the Alans as they were strung out in an effort to turn the flank.[15]

In speaking of his own troops, Arrian notes that the "Roman horsemen carry their lances and strike the enemy in the same manner as do the Alans and the Sarmatians."[16] This could not have been said about Caesar's or Augustus's cavalry, and thus it may be inferred from Arrian's remark that steppe tactics were influencing Roman cavalry tactics in a noticeable manner by the early second century. This, as well as Arrian's deliberate consideration of Alan military capabilities, reinforces the earlier impression that Westerners took the Alans' martial accomplishments seriously.

Arrian's effective defense against the Alans in Cappadocia kept

14. Arrian, *Tactica*, p. 15. Cf. the editions of Hercher and Blancard on this point. See also Arrian, *Contra Alanos*, ll. 25ff. F. H. Sandbach, "Greek Literature, Philosophy, and Science," *CAH*, XI (1936), 689; Rostovtzeff, *Iranians and Greeks*, p. 118; Mommsen, *Röm. Gesch.*, V, 405; and Alphonse Dain, "Les stratégistes Byzantins," *Travaux et Mémoires*, II (1967), 331–332. On the feigned retreat in general, see Bernard S. Bachrach, "The Feigned Retreat at Hastings," *Mediaeval Studies*, XXXIII (1971), 344–347. See appendix II.
15. Arrian, *Contra Alanos*, ll. 25ff.
16. Arrian, *Tactica*, p. 4.

9

imperial territory safe. Armenia, Rome's satellite to the north, was forced to purchase an Alan withdrawal from its territory with "gifts." Dio Cassius, whose information on these events cannot have been firsthand, seems to credit the tribute paid by the Armenian ruler Vologasus II as being of greater significance in obtaining peace than was the fear of imperial military force.[17]

Evidence of increased Western contact with and Roman respect for the Alans is echoed in a small way in one of the few surviving poems by the Emperor Hadrian, who wrote, "Borysthenes the Alan was Caesar's horse, over level land, through the swamps and over the Tuscan hills he used to fly. And never on a Pannonian boar hunt could any charging boar with whitish tusks come close to injuring him. It used to happen that saliva sprinkled from his mouth to the end of his tail in the chase. But while he was still in full youth and his legs were not yet weakened by age, he died on his birthday and was buried here in the earth."[18]

Whether the horse described in Hadrian's poem was in fact a steppe pony sent to an appreciative emperor by a victorious legate or merely a good mount whose attributes called to mind the qualities of the Alan horse cannot be ascertained. The term *Borysthenes* is clearly a reference to the Dniester River, thus indicating that Hadrian associates his Alan horse with an area considerably to the north and west of that inhabited by the Alans whom Arrian encountered in Cappadocia. In any case, Alan horses or at least awareness of their capabilities were known in the West early in the second century, and a poem by an emperor on the subject surely made those who heard it aware of the equestrian Alans.

Some relatively organized sense of where Westerners thought the Alans dwelt can be obtained from the works of the geographer Ptolemy and his near contemporary Dionysius Periegetes. Ptolemy locates Alan habitats in both Asia and Europe. For him the river Don is the boundary between the two continents, and Alans live both to the east and west of it. Those living to the west of the Don, Ptolemy calls Scythian Alans and the area in which

17. Dio Cassius, LXIX, 15. Mommsen, *Röm. Gesch.*, V, 405.
18. Hadrian, *Borysthenes Alanus*, ed. Büchner.

they live he terms European Sarmatia.[19] The Alans mentioned by Seneca and Pliny a century or so earlier were from this area. The Alans Ptolemy locates east of the Don are also called Scythian Alans and may perhaps be identified with those mentioned earlier by Josephus and Suetonius. Dionysius Periegetes, in a poem written in Greek and titled *Description of the Inhabited Earth*, claims that the Alans dwelt in the area from the Danube to the shores of the Black Sea. Thus he notices only the European Alans and ignores those in Asia.[20]

From the works of Ptolemy and Dionysius it can be seen that there were several groups of Alans living in both Asia and Europe along with many other peoples. Among the Alans' neighbors in various places were the Peucini, Bastarni, Roxolani, Iazyges, Nervii, Geloni, Getae, and Sarmatians. There is no reason to believe that the Alans dominated their neighbors, and from Ptolemy's account it is clear that the Alan habitats did not constitute a contiguous area. Between the Alans living in European Sarmatia and those in Asiatic Scythia was a huge tract of land called Asiatic Sarmatia in which, according to Ptolemy, no Alans dwelt.[21]

It should be pointed out that although the Alans did not develop an empire, they were of considerable importance. Ptolemy notes the location of the Alanus mountains which were probably

19. Ptolemy makes several references to the Alans but usually uses the term *Alauni* to describe them. This usage could lead to unfortunate confusions since the *Alauni* were a Celtic people. By using the phrase Scythian-Alauni, Ptolemy tries to avoid a measure of confusion, but for the modern reader, as probably for the ancient reader, the geographical location of these various groups of *Alauni* is perhaps of even greater help in distinguishing between Celt and Alan. The *Alauni* located in Britain, Spain, and Noricum (*Geog.*, II, 3.9; II, 6.4; II, 14.9) are Celts. Those located in European Sarmatia (*Geog.*, III, 5.15; 19.21) and in Scythia within the Imaus mountains (*Geog.*, VI, 14.3; 9.11) were Alans. See Täubler, "Alanen," p. 19; Müllenhoff, *Deutsche Altertumskunde*, III, 94; E. H. Bunbury, *A History of Ancient Geography*, 2nd ed. (London, 1883), II, 591; and M. Dillon and Nora K. Chadwick, *The Celtic Realms* (London, 1967), pp. 19, 20, 21, 23.

20. Dionysius Periegetes, ll. 302–313. Täubler, "Alanen," p. 26; Müllenhoff, *Deutsche Altertumskunde*, III, 84ff; Tomaschek, "Alanen," col. 1282; Bunbury, *Ancient Geography*, II, 486; M. I. Rostovtzeff, *Skythien und der Bosporus* (Berlin, 1931), p. 73; and Thompson, *Attila and the Huns*, pp. 20–21.

21. Ptolemy, *Geog.*, V, 8.1–32, provides no mention of the Alans. See III, 5.19, and Dionysius, ll. 302–313, for mentions of other tribes.

named for them, and Dionysius, when listing the many peoples who lived in the area from the Danube to the Black Sea, provides details only about the Alans. He calls them "mighty" and notes their outstanding equestrian abilities.[22]

The Greek writer Lucian, a contemporary of Ptolemy, provides additional information about the Alans in south Russia. Among Lucian's many works was a dialogue between a Scythian and a Greek on the subject of friendship. The dialogue, however, is merely the form chosen by Lucian to tell a story about the Scythians, a subject concerning which he was well informed. Alans are frequently mentioned in Lucian's story, and it is apparent from the context that they were well known to his audience. The Alans' fighting prowess as horsemen as well as their effective use of the spear and bow is treated as commonplace. The close relation of the Alans to the Scythians is emphasized by Lucian, who indicates that their dress and customs are very similar. In fact, according to Lucian, the only significant characteristic distinguishing the two is the way each wears his hair; the Scythians wear it longer than do the Alans.[23]

Through the remainder of the second century Westerners needed neither geographers nor poets to remind them of the Alans on the borders. In the era of the Pax Romana and later when barbarian raids kept Roman generals and emperors occupied, some Alan groups continued a westward movement. The armies of Antonius Pius, Hadrian's successor, frequently parried Alan thrusts against imperial territory.[24] Antonius's successor, Marcus Aurelius, found Alans among a huge coalition of barbarians which invaded the western part of the empire from Illyria to Gaul. Alan efforts in these campaigns seem to have been directed further west than were previous ones. Only Seneca's vague allusion to Alan raids across the Danube more than a century earlier provides prior evidence for their activities so far west.[25]

22. Ptolemy, *Geog.*, III, 5.15; VI, 14.11, and Dionysius, ll. 312–313.
23. Lucian, *Tox.*, 51. Rostovtzeff, *Skythien und der Bosporus*, I, 96–99, notes that Lucian uses background material on the steppe peoples which is reasonably accurate but that his historical and geographical data is less worthwhile.
24. *HA*, Antonius Pius, V, 5.
25. *Ibid.*, Marcus Aurelius, XXII, 1.

Among the barbarians defeated by Marcus Aurelius were the Buri. Marcus's son Commodus followed up this victory by compelling the enemy invaders to release numerous imperial prisoners and to give hostages. Commodus then forced a group of Alans, which had been part of the coalition that Marcus had defeated, to relinquish a large number of prisoners which they held. In addition, Commodus made the Alans swear an oath that they would abandon a five-mile strip of territory along the Dacian border and that they would neither inhabit this buffer zone nor use it for pasturing their herds.[26]

Alans who dwelt in the Pontic area farther to the east seem to have lived in harmony with Rome's satellites. A Greek monument from the Taman peninsula built in A.D. 208 has been discovered which bears an inscription praising the abilities of the chief Alan interpreter in the Pontic region. "Chief interpreter" suggests subordinates, which in turn implies that there was a small corps of interpreters who knew the Alan language and perhaps Greek or some other important language of the area.[27]

In the northern parts of Thrace other Alans along with Goths were being assimilated by the local populations during the latter part of the second century. The story of Maximinus the Thracian illustrates this well. Born of an Alan mother and a Gothic father in the north of Thrace bordering on the lands in which the barbarians dwelt, Maximinus spent his early youth as a herdsman. When he grew older, he became the leader of an armed band which patrolled the border and protected the village against bandits. Because of the military abilities Maximinus had demonstrated, he had no difficulty in entering the Roman cavalry, the most prestigious branch of the imperial military. He was able to do this even though he spoke Thracian and scarcely mastered Latin. In a relatively short time Maximinus rose to high command in the Roman army, but during the reign of Macrinus he retired

26. Dio Cassius, LXXIII, 3 (Bekker ed., II, 351). According to W. Tomaschek, "Borani" and "Buri," *RE*, cols. 719, 1067, both groups were German, not Sarmatian.

27. I. T. Kruglikova, *Bospor v pozdneantichnoe vremia* (Moscow, 1966), p. 54, and Ellis H. Minns, *Scythians and Greeks* (Cambridge, 1913), p. 614, n. 2.

to an estate on the Thracian border near the Danube and there carried on trading operations with the Alans and the Goths who lived across the river.[28]

There is no need to recount Maximinus's seizure of the imperial

28. *HA*, Maximinus, I, 5; II, 1, 2, 5; IV, 4, 5; IX, 3–6. See also *ibid.*, Herodian, VI, 8, 9; VII, VIII *passim*.

While scholars have generally agreed that the *HA* is a grab bag of fact and fiction, two studies by Ronald Syme, *Ammianus and the Historia Augusta* (Oxford, 1968) and *Emperors and Biography* (Oxford, 1971), have gone a long way in further reducing their credibility as useful historical sources. Syme notes that Ammianus's mentions of the Alans in the *HA* should inspire doubt in an early date for its composition and in the accuracy of the data (*Ammianus*, p. 36). Syme pursues these doubts only in the case of the Emperor Maximinus's parentage. He points out that Herodian, a more reliable source than the *HA*, indicates that Maximinus "came from the semi-savages of inner Thrace . . ." while the *HA* "transplants the natal village to the vicinity of the Danube" (*Ammianus*, p. 37). In *Emperors*, p. 184, Syme goes further and accepts as basic but with slight modification Mommsen's conclusion that whatever "does not derive from Herodian is to be discarded." Syme argues that the word *Gothia* in this episode is "surely post-Constantinian" and "should have sufficed for condemnation" (p. 182).

These specific criticisms and Syme's general reservation about the data concerning the Alans must be seen in light of his thesis that the *HA* was a product of the late fourth century and not of the first half of that century. Syme thus sets out to show that the ambiance of the late fourth century (ca. 395) permeates the *HA*. The Alans (see ch. II below) appear in the West in larger and larger numbers during the later fourth century. It is Syme's a priori assumption that they impinged noticeably upon the author's consciousness and he thus used them in making up his stories. This treatment of the Alans would be more convincing if they first began to appear in the sources during the later fourth century. We have seen, however, that a dozen and a half sources dating before 350 discuss the Alans in some detail or at least mention them. There is of course no way to ascertain how many dozens of authors whose works are no longer extant provided information about the Alans to writers in the late fourth century.

Syme's attack on the story of Maximinus's parentage is far from compelling. If the term *Gothia* was in fact anachronistic in the early third century, and it probably was, must we condemn the entire episode as fiction? Is it not possible that the author introduced this anachronism while copying a third-century source? Alans had been in the Danube area since the early first century A.D. Many scholars, as Syme admits, argue that the names given for Maximinus's parents are legitimate Alan and Gothic appellations (p. 182, n. 5). (See n. 33 below for confirmation of an apparently bizarre story found in the *HA* concerning the Alans; why does Syme ignore this episode?) Perhaps if Professor Syme were more aware of the Alans' propensity for assimilation and the range of their activities, he would not dismiss the data in the *HA* concerning them in such a cavalier manner. Were Syme to admit the general accuracy of the Alan data it would not help his thesis. But if his thesis were to rest solely upon refuting the Alan evidence, it would not be much of a thesis anyway.

14

throne and his bloody fall, but it is worth recalling that he was the first emperor to be fully barbarian. Yet his Alan or Gothic ancestry had little to do with his rise to power. He was not a barbarian ruler in the mold of an Odoacer or a Ricimer who could call upon barbarian armies for support; rather he was a "Roman" general, perhaps like a Septimus Severus, who had strong support in the imperial army. If anything Maximinus's barbarian ancestry was a handicap rather than an aid, and while he was emperor he tried to hide the facts about his origins as best he could.[29]

During the so-called crash of the third century when twenty-six emperors were recognized at Rome and all but one died a violent death, relatively little history was being written and there are few mentions of the Alans. We do learn, however, that the Alans may have forayed into Greece early in the 240s. They are said to have defeated the Emperor Gordian III on the plains of Philippi.[30] Toward the middle of the century and later, barbarian invaders harassed the Danubian provinces. Though the limited sources are mute on the Alans' involvement, it seems reasonable to surmise that at least some of those who dwelt along the borders, especially in Dacia, took part in these adventures. A late source suggests that Alans may even have raided into northern Italy and Gaul at about this time.[31] A list of captives who adorned the triumph of Aurelian in 273 partly substantiates these conjectures: "there were Goths, Alans, Roxolans, Sarmatians, Franks, Sueves, Vandals, and Germans."[32]

Probus also campaigned against the Alans, but, besides an anecdote about an Alan horse which was allegedly captured by Probus's victorious forces, nothing is known about this episode. The anecdote tells of a horse which was neither handsome nor big but had great stamina and was supposedly able to cover a

29. *HA*, Maximinus, I, 7.
30. *Ibid.*, Gordian, III, xxxiv, 4.
31. Jordanes, *Romana*, 281: "Germani et Alani Gallias depraedantes Ravennam usque venerunt."
32. *HA*, Aurelian, XXXIII, 4, 5.

hundred miles in a day and to keep up such a pace for eight or ten days.[33] From the earlier mention by Martial of the Alan's Sarmatian horse through the notice of Alan equestrian ability by Arrian and Dionysius Periegetes, and Hadrian's praise of the Alan horse, the steppe pony had begun to assume almost legendary attributes in the West by the latter part of the fourth century.

The restoration of relative peace and order in the empire by Diocletian did not bring with it a revival of secular historical writing — at least nothing of importance from that period has survived. From the early dominate only a few notices of the Alans are extant. Julius Valerius, who translated the pseudo-Callisthenes into Latin, adds the Alans to a list of peoples named by his source. Whereas the pseudo-Callisthenes mentions the Scythians, Arabs, Oxydrakes, Iberians, Seres, Daucones, Dapates, Bosphorians, Agroi, Zalboi, Chaldeans, Mesopotamians, Agroiphagi, and the Euonyitae, Julius omits the Dapates, Bosporians, Agroi, Zalboi, Chaldeans, and the Mesopotamians in his "translation" and adds to it Indians, Phoenicians, Parthians, Assyrians, and Alans. Where the pseudo-Callisthenes considers those people he cites to be "great nations of the East," Julius calls those in his list "barbarians."[34]

Hegesippus's rendition of Josephus's *Jewish Wars* is another Latin translation of a Greek work which differs from the original with regard to the Alans. Where Josephus describes the Alans as a Scythian people about whom he had previously commented, Hegesippus terms the Alans a "fierce people" who for a long time were not known in the West.[35] Festus Rufus Avienus's Latin version of Dionysius Periegetes's Greek poem on the earth and its people also varies from the original in its treatment of the Alans. While Dionysius depicts the Alans as a mighty people and notes their equestrian abilities, Avienus is content to call them fierce.[36]

The *Tabula Peutingeria*, a map of sorts from this period, places

33. *Ibid.*, Probus, VIII, 3. T. Peisker, "The Asiatic Background," *CMH*, I (1911), 331–332, calls attention to the Turkoman horses which can cover 650 miles in five days.

34. Pseudo-Callisthenes, I, 2, and Julius Valerius, I, 1.

35. Hegesippus, L.

36. Avienus, *Orb. Terr.*, ll. 436–445.

16

the Alans north of the Black Sea living among the Nervii and the Aspergiani.[37] Though none of these jejune notices provide information on contemporary Alan activities, they do indicate continued Western interest in this group. The altering of old texts to include information about the Alans and the introduction of Alans into material which made no mention of them illustrate this continued interest and the Alans' continued importance.

The apparent ignorance in the West of what the Alans were doing during the early dominate may be explained partly by the lack of contemporary historical narratives of a secular nature. Consideration, however, should also be given to the political conditions of the time. The Alans who had been settled within the empire as well as those who dwelt along the borders (like the stock from which the Emperor Maximinus was descended) were far along the road to assimilation. For example, those of Maximinus's generation did not speak Gothic or Alan but rather the local Thracian patois, and some, like the emperor himself, learned Latin. Those Alans beyond the borders of the empire who were not being assimilated in a more peaceful manner persisted in raiding and plundering. However, they were dealt a number of crippling defeats in the decade preceding Diocletian's accession, and thus they were in a poor position to continue serious raiding operations against imperial territory. In addition, the victories over the Alans by Aurelian and Probus were shortly followed by Diocletian's military reforms which strengthened the frontier defenses.

The paucity of available information for the first three centuries of Alan relations with the West is compensated for, to some degree, by the observations of Ammianus Marcellinus. He brings together much of what was thought to have been known about the Alans and tries to make sense of these data. In addition, he campaigned throughout the eastern part of the empire and may well have had direct contact with Alans; at the very least it can be assumed that he knew people who had observed various Alan groups.

37. *Tabula Peutingeriana, Segmentum,* IX.

Ammianus maintains that the Alans, whom he locates beyond the Danube, took their name from the Alanus mountains of European Sarmatia; this information also appears in the work of Ptolemy. Ammianus goes on to say that the Alans "inhabit the measureless wastelands of Scythia" and that they roam from the Sea of Azov to the Cimmerian Bosporus through Media and Armenia. He also talks of Alans in Scythia who dwell in the region of the Imaus mountains.[38]

Ammianus may have been wrong in his assumption that the Alans were named after the Alanus mountains, for we cannot ascertain whether these mountains in fact had such a name before people called Alans had come so far west. Ammianus was not too well informed about Alans in the East either; this, however, is understandable since he was an inhabitant of the Roman empire.

The Alans, according to Ammianus, conquered many peoples and assimilated them. Among these people were Nervii, Vidiani, Geloni, and Agathyrisi. Included among the Alans' neighbors were Melanchlaenae and Anthropophagai as well as Amazons. This list of peoples, some mythical, some very ancient, and others contemporary, should not mislead the reader into rejecting Ammianus's main point, i.e., the Alans were formed from a mélange of different peoples. He writes, "Thus the Alans . . . though widely separated from each other and roaming over great areas, as do nomads, in the course of time have united under one name, and are called Alans because of the similarity in their customs, their savage way of life, and their weapons."[39]

38. Ammianus Marcellinus, XXXI, 2, 12, 13, 16, 21; XXII, 8, 31, 38, 42; XXIII, 6, 61. Ammianus's suggestion that the Alans were in earlier times called Massagetae is based on Dio Cassius, LXIX, 15, who in turn seems to be relying on Lucan. See Sanford, "Nero and the East," p. 98, n. 2; P. Herrmann, "Massagetai," *RE*, cols. 2124–2129. Our main source for the Massagetae is Herodotus from whom we learn that they were matriarchal in their social structure. See Sulimirski, *Sarmatians*, pp. 55–61. This alone would seem to make any close connection between the Massagetae and the *Alani* unlikely. For the position of women among the latter, see below, pp. 20–21. For a defense of Ammianus's accuracy on the Alans see E. A. Thompson, *The Historical Work of Ammianus Marcellinus* (Cambridge, 1947), p. 119.

39. Ammianus Marcellinus, XXXI, 2, 13–17: "Hi bipertiti per utramque mundi plagam Halani, quorum gentes varias nunc recensere non refert, licet

18

It is safe to conclude from Ammianus's remarks that the Alans were a cultural entity composed of many peoples and not simply a linguistic or "racial" group. It was the presence of certain customs which created in the minds of observers, and perhaps for the Alans themselves, an identity. Despite the composite nature of the Alans, Ammianus goes so far as to say that "almost all of the Alans are tall and good looking, their hair is generally blond."[40] He further indicates that the Alans inspire fear by the ferocity of their glance. Nevertheless, it is difficult to accept this claim of general physiognomical homogeneity if one is to accept also the diverse origins of those called Alans. This physical description of the Alans may have applied to the "original" Alans or to a particular group of Alans concerning which Ammianus had some detailed information. It is more likely, however, that Ammianus was striving in this instance to distinguish the Alans from the Huns in a significant manner. At first he notes that the Alans and the Huns are similar in many ways but then he goes on to describe the latter as short, misshapen, and ugly.[41]

The Alans are pictured in Western accounts as primitive nomads. They lived in wooden wagons covered with bark canopies and drawn by draft cattle. All the private activities of the nuclear family were carried on within these wagons. The Alans drove herds of horses and cattle and flocks of sheep along with them as they roamed from camp to camp. The cattle and sheep provided meat and milk which were the mainstays of their diet. Wild fruit was used as a supplement. Further dietary needs were satisfied through hunting, which played an important role in their economic and social life. From hunting both meat and skins were obtained as well as bone, horn, and teeth which were used for tools, ornaments, and fuel.[42]

dirempti spatiis longis, per pagos (ut Nomades) vagantur immensos, aevi tamen progressu, ad unum concessere vocabulum, et summatim omnes Halani cognominantur, ob mores et modum efferatum vivendi, eandemque armaturam."
40. *Ibid.*, XXX, 2, 21.
41. *Ibid.*, XXXI, 2, 1–3.
42. *Ibid.*, XXXI, 2, 18, 19. I think it is too dangerous to generalize further from these limited sources or from evidence relating to other nomadic peoples who inhabited the same areas as did the Alans and who were

A History of the Alans

To find suitable pasturage land for their herds the Alans moved frequently, so frequently in fact that they did not even build crude huts, but made their wagons their permanent homes. When a stop was made, the Alans circled their wagons, probably as a defensive measure, and set their animals out to graze. The Alans preferred to camp along rivers not only because of the easily available water but because the lush grass on the river banks made for good pasturage for their animals. In addition, wild fruit was probably more available along the river banks than in dryer places. As is common among nomads, the Alans did not cultivate the soil, or have any formal ownership of land. The dependence upon herds, which is intrinsic to steppe nomadism, keeps any such group of people from becoming very large. Relatively few nomadic herders wander over vast tracts of land in search of fodder for their animals.[43]

The Alans' primitive material culture is mirrored in their social structure. The society seems to have been divided into two parts on the basis of the division of labor; those who fought and hunted constituted one group, and those who did not engage in these activities formed the other group. The latter segment comprised women, children, and old men, and its position in the society seems to have been relatively humble. Old men were scorned because they had survived and had not died in battle — apparently that was the only honorable way to die.[44] From a later source it can be inferred that the Alans were polygamous;[45] this might also have contributed to limiting the influence of women in society. According to a contemporary, slavery as it was known by Westerners in the classical world was not practiced by the Alans.[46] This suggests that the women, children, and old men

in a similar "stage" of development. See my review of Sergei I. Rudenko, *The Frozen Tombs of Siberia,* AHR, LXXVI (1971), 754. Cf. Thompson, *Attila and the Huns,* pp. 43–46.
43. Ammianus Marcellinus, XXXI, 2, 18, 19.
44. *Ibid.,* XXXI, 2, 20.
45. Salvian, *De gub. Dei,* VII, 15: "Gothorum gens perfida, sed pudica est, Alanorum impudica, sed minus perfida. . . ." See J. M. Wallace-Hadrill, *The Long-Haired Kings* (London, 1962), p. 161, and Bernard S. Bachrach, "The Alans in Gaul," *Traditio,* XXIII (1967), 486.
46. Ammianus Marcellinus, XXXI, 2, 25: "Servitus quid sit ignorant . . ." See Thompson, *Attila and the Huns,* p. 22.

performed whatever labor was necessary. They tended the wagons, cooked, and carried out any other light work essential to sustaining the domestic elements of their materially primitive existence. Artisans as a group are not mentioned in the sources.

The absence of slavery among the Alans raises the question of what they did with their captives. We know that they were not averse to returning important captives for ransom, but what about the others?[47] It is possible that the Alans practiced a kind of ritual adoption. Lucian, who knew a great deal about these peoples, remarks on the great similarities between the Scythians and the Alans and notes that the former engaged in a practice that modern anthropologists would classify as ritual adoption.[48] The integration of prisoners of war into the families or clans of the captors is not infrequently practiced by nomadic peoples. This custom would have been facilitated by the heterogeneous nature of the Alan people, composed as they were of many diverse tribes and groups. It may be suggested that the assimilation of captives by the Alans was in microcosm simply the counterpart of how they treated entire peoples on a larger scale.[49]

Politically, all fighting men among the Alans were regarded as worthy of playing a leadership role. The leaders, apparently at every level, were chosen from among those warriors most experienced in combat. Whether family relationships or other considerations impinged upon this process of political selection cannot be ascertained. It is clear, however, that the Alans did not have councils of elders as did their German contemporaries. While the Germanic peoples are said to have venerated their aged men as wise, the Alans scorned theirs as cowardly and degenerate.[50]

Religion was one of the institutions that provided the diverse peoples called Alans with their identity. Like other elements of Alan life, this too was relatively simple. According to Ammianus, the Alans had no permanent shrines or temples and apparently no formal priesthood of any kind. They worshipped a symbol of

47. See n. 7 above.
48. George Vernadsky, *The Origins of Russia* (Oxford, 1959), pp. 13ff.
49. Ammianus Marcellinus, XXXI, 2, 17.
50. *Ibid.*, XXXI, 2, 25.

sorts—a naked sword thrust into the bare earth. The sword (and it is unclear if any sword was adequate or if there was a special one) seems to have represented the god of war who in Latin was called Mars. This god of war is the only god concerning which we have information, and may indeed have been their only god. He is said to have been the god who presided over all the lands over which the Alans roamed as well as the god of war. The worship of the god of war was common among the steppe barbarians during the fourth century as was the sword symbol.[51]

A later source notes that the Alans worshipped or, perhaps more exactly, venerated their ancestors. This is consistent with general steppe practices and with the Alan beliefs as they are described by Ammianus. The ancestors presumably died somewhere on the lands over which their descendants wandered. The "happy dead" among the Alans, i.e., those who had died in battle while serving the god of war on his lands, would be worthy of veneration by their descendants who were biased toward instilling martial values and maintaining them.[52]

The Alans also took a strong interest in predicting the future or at least in obtaining omens concerning it. At specific times, perhaps when preparing to move to a new area, certain people, whose identity and status we do not know, gathered a bundle of straight twigs of osier wood and dropped the bundle on a bed of sand while reciting certain incantations. From the pattern formed by the twigs scattered on the sand the person performing the ritual predicted or, more precisely, read the future. This ritual, like ancestor veneration, has definite oriental parallels,

51. *Ibid.*, XXXI, 2, 22, 23. Thompson, *Atilla and the Huns*, p. 89, notes that the Huns believed in a god of war who had a sacred sword. E. A. Thompson, *The Visigoths in the Time of Ulfila* (Oxford, 1966), p. 60.

52. Claudius Marius Victor, *Alethia*, III, ll. 189–193: "facinus plus inquinat istud,/ quod speciem virtutis habet; nam protinus omnes/ amplexae gentes scelus hoc sine fine litantes/ manibus inferias, uti nunc testantur Alani,/ pro dis quaeque suis caros parentes. . . ." Ancestor veneration was also practiced by the Alans' Visigothic neighbors (Thompson, *Time of Ulfila*, p. 59) as well as by the Chinese beyond the steppes. See Täubler, "Alanen," p. 22, and Tomaschek, "Alanen," col. 1284, for Alan contacts with the Chinese. See also D. H. Smith, *Chinese Religions* (London, 1968), for ancestor veneration.

and it is known that some Alan groups had contacts with the Chinese before moving west.[53]

Because Alan society was basically militarily oriented, boys were trained in horsemanship at an early age, and the Alan fighting man even regarded going about on foot as somehow degrading. The breeding of horses was of special interest to the Alans, and we have seen that their mounts were well appreciated in the West. As indicated above, the Alans chose their chief from among the most experienced warriors, their deity was a god of war, and his symbol was a naked sword thrust into the ground. Men who died in war were regarded as having died happily and seem to have been venerated by their descendants. Those men who lived until they could no longer fight were despised as degenerates and cowards.

Armaments and military tactics were other aspects of society which apparently gave the various peoples who formed the Alans their identity. Arrian's description of the rapid cavalry movements of the Alan horsemen, their ability to strike, retreat, wheel, and strike again is noted and expanded upon by Ammianus and later contemporaries. Ammianus tells us that the military customs of the Alans closely resembled those of the Huns. Concerning the latter, he wrote, "They enter battle drawn up in wedge-shaped masses, while their medley of voices makes a savage noise. And they are lightly equipped for swift motion, and unexpected action, they purposely divide suddenly into scattered bands and attack, rushing about in disorder here and there, dealing terrific slaughter; and because of their extraordinary rapidity of movement . . . they fight from a distance with missiles . . . they gallop over the intervening spaces and fight hand to hand with swords."[54]

The Alans, too, raised a terrifying yell when they charged into battle, and, like the Huns, they also used the lasso. The mobility of Alan tactics as indicated by Arrian and Lucian and as echoed

53. Ammianus Marcellinus, XXXI, 2, 24. For Chinese divination, see R. Wilhelm, *The I Ching*, 2 vols. (London, 1951). Osier wood is of the willow family, and willows are often found in damp areas along river banks.
54. Ammianus Marcellinus, XXXI, 2, 8, 9.

by Ammianus's remark that "they are light and active in the use of arms" can be seen especially in the feigned retreat tactic. As mentioned previously, Arrian thought that the Alans' use of the feigned retreat, which was a common steppe tactic used frequently by the Huns as well, was especially dangerous.[55] In this chapter some three centuries of Western observations on the Alans have been described and discussed. Westerners describe the Alans as dwelling throughout central Asia and south Russia. While the modern reader might find this confusing, it is indicative of the nomadic nature of Alan society and its fragmentary political organization. Some Western perceptions of the Alans were probably inaccurate, as is exemplified by Ammianus's contention that they took their name from the Alanus mountains. Another example is his assertion that the Alans were tall, blond, and handsome. Although other remarks about the Alans seem to be wild exaggerations, they may in fact be true. The supposition that they stripped off the skins of their slain enemies as a spoil of war and used them for horse trappings seems to be one of those stories told to scare little children.[56] Yet when we recall that it was customary in some primitive societies to take scalps and shrink heads, it is difficult to dismiss the Alans' alleged atrocities as prejudiced inventions of hostile observers.

A very important aspect of Alan society is the pattern it developed for the assimilation of outsiders. Not only did entire tribes become Alan, but individuals who were captured in war were apparently adopted by their captors rather than used as slaves. Alans were also willing to be assimilated by other peoples. On the borders of Thrace, Alans abandoned their nomadic way of life to settle down in villages and even learned the local language, apparently at the expense of giving up their own. Yet even when they settled down and intermarried with other peoples, the Alans' heritage of equestrian prowess and animal herding survived.

It may be dangerous to draw too many specific conclusions from

55. *Ibid.*, XXXI, 2, 21; Claudian, *De Cons. Stilic.*, XXI, l. 109. Bernard S. Bachrach, "The Origin of Armorican Chivalry," *Technology and Culture*, X (1969), 167–168.
56. Ammianus Marcellinus, XXXI, 2, 22.

the limited sources, but it seems reasonable to suggest that the Alans beyond the borders of the empire were tough and able mounted warriors whose society was materially primitive, nomadic, and organized for war. Culturally the Alans had developed patterns of assimilation which facilitated their absorption of conquered peoples as well as their own ability to be assimilated by other cultures. Such assimilation occurred when the Alans moved westward into the Roman empire.

CHAPTER II

The Alans
Come to the West

WHEN the Huns burst upon the steppes of south Russia early in the 370s, among the first peoples they encountered were the Alans. For several years bands of Alans and Huns fought a war of raiding, burning each other's camps and stealing or scattering each other's herds. Ultimately, the Alans were worn down by this almost constant warfare, and the Huns emerged as the dominant power on the steppes. Among those Alan bands which survived, some fled westward while others were made subjects of the Huns.[1]

Some groups of Alans along with several bands of Huns moved against the Ostrogoths whose lands were between them and the Roman empire. When Ermanrich, the Ostrogothic king, saw the danger facing his people, he committed suicide. He was succeeded by Vithimiris who was able to secure the aid of a band of Huns to help fight the invaders. The Alan-Hun forces, however, were able to defeat the Gothic-Hun forces in a series of hard-fought battles. Vithimiris was killed in the last of these encounters, and two war leaders, Alatheus and Saphrax, assumed control of the Goths' affairs. The latter, Saphrax, is generally re-

---

1. Ammianus Marcellinus, XXXI, 2, 12; 3, 1; and Jordanes, *Getica*, XXIX. Jordanes seems to have obtained his information on this point from Priscus. See Thompson, *Attila and the Huns*, p. 22.

garded as having an Alan name. In any event, this group of Goths moved southward toward the Roman frontier.[2]

By 376, large numbers of steppe peoples, mostly Visigoths, were trying to cross into imperial territory. Roman officials permitted some to enter the empire; other groups crossed the borders without the benefit of permission. For the most part, these immigrants were maltreated by imperial officials who robbed them of their riches, extorted exorbitant prices for food, and carried off young boys and women to their beds.[3]

Some barbarian groups responded to this abuse by banding together for the purpose of despoiling the empire. A large group of Alans, Goths, and Huns joined forces to plunder imperial territory in Thrace. Other Alans, operating in *Dacia Ripensis*, attacked the Emperor Gratian who was on his way to the East to help Valens deal with the barbarian invaders. Yet another group of Alans joined the Goths led by Fritigern and those led by Alatheus and Saphrax, these two Gothic groups having united a short time earlier. These barbarian forces met the army of the Emperor Valens near Adrianople in 378 and defeated it decisively. The key blow of the battle was struck by a force of Alan and Gothic cavalry which caught the Roman flank by surprise and threw it into confusion. After the battle of Adrianople, in which Valens lost his life and the East Roman field army was shattered, more Alans united with the victors. These groups, along with a band of Huns which also joined up after Adrianople, tried unsuccessfully to seize Constantinople.[4]

It would not be wholly accurate, however, to conclude that all the steppe peoples and especially the Alans who entered the empire grouped together as a matter of policy to ravage Roman lands. For battles between the various barbarian groups were not infrequent: Goths fought amongst themselves, and against

2. Ammianus Marcellinus, XXXI, 3, 1ff. On Saphrax, or as it is sometimes rendered Safrac, see Ludwig Schmidt, *Geschichte der deutsche Stämme*, I (Berlin, 1910), 108, 112, 114, 168, 173, and Thompson, *Attila and the Huns*, pp. 23ff.

3. Ammianus Marcellinus, XXXI, 4, 1ff. E. A. Thompson, "The Visigoths from Fritigern to Euric," *Historia*, XV (1963), 105ff.

4. Ammianus Marcellinus, XXXI, 8, 4; 2, 6; 12, 1ff; 16, 3.

A HISTORY OF THE ALANS

Alans and Huns; the Alans and Huns in turn fought against each other, in union with the Goths and singly. In addition, some Alans were recruited for imperial service by the Emperor Gratian who, with Alans among his forces, was attacked by other Alans.[5] These confusing temporary alliances tend to emphasize the chaotic state of affairs caused by the onslaught of the Huns.

ALANS AND VISIGOTHS

Among the Visigoths who followed Fritigern and his successors, there was an important group of Alans. These were the same Alans who had carried out the cavalry charge at Adrianople which determined the outcome of the battle.[6] When Fritigern was succeeded by Alaric, the Alans continued to play a noteworthy role in the Visigoths' plans. In Alaric's numerous struggles against Stilicho, the Alans are singled out on at least one occasion by a contemporary as an important element of the Visigothic military.[7] In 409–410, when Alaric's forces threatened the Campania and ultimately took and sacked Rome, Paulinus of Nola, whose monastery was menaced, feared the Goths and their Alan allies equally, dreading to live in subjection to the "fierce Alani."[8]

It should be pointed out that most of these activities of the Goths and Alans were chronicled by the sixth-century writer Jordanes, a Goth who praised the Goths' accomplishments but harbored an anti-Alan bias. Thus, aside from Jordanes's accounts, what we know about the Alans who accompanied the Visigoths comes largely from sources whose primary interest is neither the Goths nor the Alans. For example, Ammianus Marcellinus pro-

5. Orosius, *Hist.*, VII, 37; Ambrose, *Expos. in Luc.*, X, 10; Ammianus Marcellinus, XXXI, 3, 1ff. C. Courtois, *Les Vandales et l'Afrique* (Paris, 1955), p. 40.
6. Ammianus Marcellinus, XXXI, 12, 1ff.
7. Claudian, *De Cons. Stilic.*, I, ll. 106ff.
8. Paulinus of Nola, *Carm.*, XXVI, ll. 22–27. Cf. Pierre Courcelle, *Histoire littéraire des grandes invasions germaniques* (Paris, 1948), p. 216, and P. Fabre, *Essai sur la chronologie de l'oeuvre de saint Paulin* (Paris, 1948), p. 113, who suggest 402, when Alaric and his Alan followers were in northern Italy, as the date for this poem.

28

vides the information on the key role played by the Alan cavalry at Adrianople, yet his main stress is upon the impact of the battle on the empire.[9]

Not until 414 did the Alans' importance within the Visigothic forces become manifest. In that year, the Visigothic King Athaulf led his followers into southern Gaul in search of a place to settle. They gained control of Narbonne, Toulouse, and Bordeaux. At Bazas, however, the Visigoths and their Alan allies were checked. Count Paulinus of Pella, a friend of the Alan leader, was besieged at Bazas along with many of his family. Paulinus ventured out of the beleaguered city to speak with the Alan chief in the hope that he might be allowed to escape with his family. Although the Alan leader could not consent to this request, he did indicate to Paulinus that he was willing to devise a plan which would raise the siege. The details were worked out; Paulinus promised the Alans land on which to settle, and the Alan leader sent his own wife and his favorite son into Bazas as hostages. Paulinus was permitted to return to the city, and the Alans with their women, children, and wagons defected from the Goths and deployed in a ring around the walls of the town.[10]

The Goths, deprived of their Alan allies, broke off the siege. Constant harassment by Constantius, the Roman military commander in Gaul, forced the Goths to flee from southern Gaul. They crossed the Pyrenees and entered Spain in 415.[11]

The Alans who had defected from the Goths did so in return

9. Ammianus Marcellinus, XXXI, 12, 1ff. On Jordanes's bias see Bernard S. Bachrach, "The Alans in Gaul," p. 483, and Ulf Täckholm, "Aetius and the Battle on the Catalaunian Fields," *Opuscula Romana*, VII (1969), 259, 263. See also n. 96 below. See N. Wagner, *Getica* (Berlin, 1967), pp. 15ff, on Jordanes and the Alans.

10. Paulinus of Pella, *Eucharisticos*, ll. 328–398. For a discussion of the land division and the text as a whole, see Bachrach, "Alans in Gaul," p. 479; Courtois, *Les Vandales*, p. 47, n. 3. Cf. W. Levison, "Bischof Germanus von Auxerre und die Quellen zu seiner Geschichte," *Neues Archiv der Gesellschaft für ältere deutsche Geschichtskunde*, XXIX (1903), 135–136. On the land division, see F. Lot, "Du régime de hospitalité," *RBPH*, VII (1928), 1007, n. 6.

11. E. A. Thompson, "The Settlement of the Barbarians in Southern Gaul," *JRS*, XLVI (1956), 65–75, and Bernard S. Bachrach, "Another Look at the Barbarian Settlement in Southern Gaul," *Traditio*, XXV (1969), 355–356.

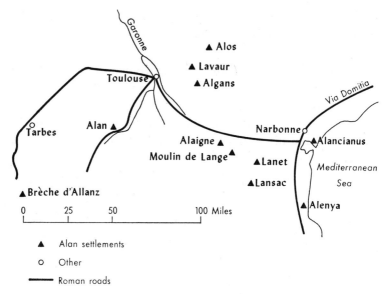

Map 1. Southwestern Gaul

for the promise that they would receive lands on which they could settle. Constantius, as part of his plan to confine the Goths in Spain, fulfilled the agreement that Paulinus had made with the Alans. A division of the land was arranged in the area between Toulouse and the Mediterranean so that the Alans could control the coastal roads, particularly the *Via Domitia* which connected Gaul and Spain. In this area Alan military settlers or their descendants appear to have given their name to the towns of Alancianus (Aude), which no longer exists but which was about three miles southeast of Narbonne; Alenya (Pyrénées-Orientales), about twenty-five miles northwest of Elne; Lanet (Aude), about twelve miles due north of Lansac; Alaigne (Aude), about twenty-five miles northwest of Lanet; and Alan (Haute-Garonne), about sixty miles west-northwest of Alaigne (see map 1).[12]

12. On the land division, Paulinus of Pella, *Eucharisticos,* ll. 395–398: "Cuius non sero secuti/ exemplum et nostri, quos diximus, auxiliares/ discessere, fidem pacis servare parati/ Romanis, quoquo ipsos sors oblata tulisset." Lot, "Hospitalité," p. 1007, n. 6, and Bachrach, "Alans in Gaul," p.

There were two strong factions among the Visigoths with whom these Alans had been allied; one group had sworn to oppose the empire, to the death if necessary, while the other was willing to benefit from Roman civilization and to serve the empire. King Athaulf, a leader of the latter persuasion, is said to have remarked frequently that early in his career he had desired to erase the Roman name and turn *Romania* into *Gothia*. But experience had taught him that the barbarism of the Goths made *Gothia* impossible and thus he decided to restore Roman greatness with the aid of Gothic arms.[13]

Soon after Athaulf's Alan allies chose *Romania* over *Gothia*, he was assassinated and Wallia, a leader of the faction hostile to Rome, succeeded him as king. It does not seem too extreme to suggest that the Alans who defected at Bazas held the balance of power between the two Gothic factions, and that their pro-Roman feelings enabled Athaulf and before him Alaric to hold the dominant position. Not only did the Alans choose to join the empire but their defection seems to have sounded Athaulf's death knell and allowed for the dominance of the faction which had sworn to oppose the empire to the death.[14]

Within a decade or so after the Alans' settlement in southern Gaul, their religious customs were commented on by Claudius Marius Victor, a rhetorician from nearby Marseilles. In his poem *Alethia*, he digresses from his commentary on Genesis to talk about "primitive" religions. He remarks that the making of sacrifices to the spirits of one's ancestors, which he characterizes as an element of Alan religion, is even more primitive than the poly-

479. On the place names, see Bachrach, "Southern Gaul," pp. 355–356; Albert Grenier, *Manuel d'archéologie Gallo-romaine*, VI. 1 (Paris, 1934), 406, and appendix III, nos. 17, 26, 51, 53, 5, 16, respectively. See also appendix III, no. 50.

13. Thompson, "Fritigern to Euric," p. 105ff. For Athaulf's sentiments, see Orosius, *Hist.*, VII, 43.

14. Thompson, "Fritigern to Euric," pp. 114–115. Sigeric usurped power for a short time after Athaulf's death but he was murdered and Wallia was elected in the acceptable manner. Concerning Wallia, Thompson remarks: "Wallia was chosen . . . precisely because the bulk of the Visigoths were convinced that he would put an end to such peace as existed with Rome . . . " (p. 115). This is almost a direct rendering of Orosius, *Hist.*, VII, 47.

theism of the Greeks and the Romans.[15] It may be surmised that these Alans, though they had been allied with the Goths for more than three decades, had not accepted the Arian Christianity of their Germanic comrades. It is of equal importance to note that while Claudius does not approve of the Alans' religion he is not in any other way critical of them. This tends to be the attitude displayed by orthodox Christians at this time toward pagans. Claudius's viewpoint also suggests that the Alans kept their promise to Count Paulinus that they would preserve the peace wherever they were settled. Thus in the quarter century after their settlement in the area between Toulouse and the Mediterranean, the Alans remained loyal supporters of the empire, enjoying the benefits of the imperial hospitality system; their Visigothic neighbors and former allies, however, occasionally violated their treaties with Rome. Thus when Aetius, the military commander in Gaul, was deprived of his Hunnic support in approximately 439, he turned to the Alans for additional aid.[16]

In 440 the Alan chief Sambida agreed to settle on deserted lands in the Valentinois along the Rhone River. It can be assumed that these Alans were drawn from the settlements between the Mediterranean and Toulouse since these Alans lived closest to what would become the new Rhone settlements. The place names Allan, Alançon, and Alençon, all in the département of Drôme and all to the south of Valence within a radius of forty-five miles, indicate the continuance of Alan influence throughout the early Middle Ages.[17]

These Alans living in the Valentinois not only helped to control the *bacaudae* in southern Gaul, but also guarded against Visigothic eastward expansion. In addition, they assisted in pro-

15. Claudius Marius Victor, *Alethia*, ll. 189–200. See Courcelle, *Histoire*, p. 221. Werner, *Attila-Reiches*, p. 16, provides evidence for an Alan burial at Marseilles.

16. Thompson, *Attila and the Huns*, p. 77; Thompson, "Southern Gaul," p. 67; and Bachrach, "Southern Gaul," p. 357.

17. *Chron. Gall.*, ch. 124: "Deserta Valentinae urbis rura Alanis, quibus Sambida praeerat, partienda tradunter." Bachrach, "Southern Gaul," pp. 354ff, and "Alans in Gaul," pp. 480–481. For place names, see appendix III, nos. 38, 18, 25, respectively.

tecting the westward approaches to the Alps and Italy.[18] In 457 the Emperor Majorian raised a contingent of Alans in Gaul, probably from the Valentinois, for his campaign against the Vandals in Spain.[19] After his defeat by the Vandals, these Alans under their new leader Beogar began raiding in southern Gaul and threatened to invade northern Italy. While on his way to oppose them, Majorian was murdered at Tortona. The Alans entered Italy and harassed the northern parts until they were defeated by Ricimer, a Visigoth and the power behind the imperial throne. Beogar was killed in this battle which took place at Bergamo in 464.[20] The remnants of Beogar's forces either settled among the Alans already living in northern Italy or returned to Gaul.

ALANS IN ITALY

When the Alans came west, some of them were recruited for military service by the Emperor Gratian. He acquired the support of these Alans with large gifts of gold and kept them loyal with preferential treatment. By favoring his Alan fighting men, however, Gratian alienated his other troops who ultimately revolted and killed him.[21]

Theodosius I, who ruled the entire empire after Gratian's death, was also able to recruit Alans for imperial military service. Some of these Alans may have been taken first as prisoners, for Theodosius campaigned against the Alans frequently and was generally successful. According to one contemporary, the sight of bound Alan prisoners was not uncommon in the cities of Italy.[22]

It seems likely that at least some of the Alans who had served

18. Thompson, "Southern Gaul," p. 67, and Bachrach, "Southern Gaul," p. 357. On the roads, see Grenier, *Manuel d'archéologie*, VI. 1, pls. I, II.

19. Sidonius Apollinaris, *Carm.*, 5, ll. 474–478. For a defense of the reliability of this text, see Bernard S. Bachrach, "A Note on Alites," *Byzantinische Zeitschrift*, LXV (1968), 35.

20. Jordanes, *Getica*, XLV; Marcellinus Comes, *Chron.*, 464; and *Fasti Vind. priores*, ch. 593.

21. *Ep. de Caes.*, ch. 47, and Zosimus, IV, 35.

22. Bede, *Chron.*, p. 298; Orosius, *Hist.*, VII, 34; Marcellinus Comes, *Chron.*, 379; Pacatus, *Pan. Lat.*, XX, xi, xxxii; Ausonius, *Ephemeris*, IV, 7, ll. 17–18; and Jerome, *Epist.*, LX, 16.

under Gratian and under Theodosius remained in imperial service in the West under Honorius, the latter's successor. In 401, Stilicho, Honorius's military commander and the power behind the throne, led a force against the Visigothic King Alaric who had invaded Italy. When Stilicho met Alaric's army at Pollentia, he allotted the key role in his battle plan to a troop of Alans. The Alan chief, who though a pagan had taken the name of Saul, may even have been the field commander for the entire operation. In any case, Saul was apparently rash or overzealous in carrying out his part in the maneuver, for although Alaric was defeated he was able to escape capture because the Alans failed to cut off his retreat.[23]

This battle marked the third time in half a decade that Stilicho's forces had defeated Alaric, as well as the third time that the Gothic leader had avoided capture. Rumors were rife that not only Stilicho but also the Alan chief, who apparently had permitted Alaric to escape, was disloyal to the empire. That other Alans were an important group of fighting men in Alaric's army lent additional support to the charges leveled at Saul and his troops.[24]

When Alaric once again invaded Italy, Stilicho called upon his Alan forces for support. They, however, had become somewhat resentful of the slurs upon their trustworthiness. Yet the Alan chief, whose loyalty was in question, had taught his men that they were now subjects of Rome and urged them to fight and if necessary to give up their lives for the empire.[25]

23. Claudian, De Con. Hon. VI, ll. 223ff; Orosius, Hist., VII, 37. See E. Demougeot, De l'unité à la division de l'empire romain, 395–410 (Paris, 1951), pp. 275–276. Cf. Alan Cameron, Claudian, Poetry and Propaganda at the Court of Honorius (Oxford, 1970), pp. 181, 374–377, who delves unconvincingly into the propaganda issue. The proper focus in the matter of propaganda should be the work of the pro-Gothic historians like Cassiodorus a century later. The work of these men has distorted the whole picture. See the brief observation by Täckholm, "Catalaunian Fields," p. 263.

24. Claudian, De Bel. Goth., ll. 580ff; De Cons. Stilic., I, ll. 106ff. Cf. Cameron, Claudian, p. 181.

25. Claudian, De Bel. Goth., ll. 580ff. Cf. Cameron, Claudian, p. 181, and the observations of N. H. Baynes, "A Note on Professor Bury's 'History of the Later Roman Empire,'" JRS, XII (1922), 207–210, concerning the chronology of the battles.

Stilicho not only trusted these Alans but gave them an important role in the battle of Verona against Alaric. The Alan leader Saul, described by a contemporary as a little scarred warrior with fierce, blazing eyes and a heroic visage, commanded one of the flanks of the Roman army and led a charge against the Goths. His death in the thickest of the battle acquitted him of any lingering charges of treachery. According to Claudian, the chief's death so disconcerted his troops that they retreated. This retreat threatened to expose Stilicho's flank to a Gothic counterattack. Stilicho, however, brought up a force of infantry which, with the support of the "quickly rallied" Alan horsemen, held the line successfully.[26] The possibility that the Alan retreat at Verona was simply another instance of the feigned retreat tactic should not be overlooked. The feigned retreat is especially probable in this case in light of the Alans' rapid recovery and the close and successful manner in which they coordinated their actions with Stilicho's infantry.[27]

Despite the loss of their chief, who had so well demonstrated his loyalty to Rome, the Alans settled in Italy continued to serve the empire. In 405, when a horde of barbarians threatened to invade Italy, Stilicho once again found his Alan troops willing and able to play a significant role in the defense of their new homeland.[28]

The Alans who formed such a prominent element in Stilicho's army were not just mercenaries; they were committed to the idea of becoming a part of the empire. As a contemporary somewhat poetically commented, "Alans, you have adopted the customs of Latium."[29] This is noteworthy not only because of the Alans' efforts to become a part of the Roman world, but also because it is yet another example of the pattern of assimilation observed by Westerners as a characteristic of the Alans when they were

26. Claudian, De Bel. Goth., ll. 580ff, and Demougeot, L'empire romain, pp. 278–281.
27. Bachrach, "Feigned Retreat," pp. 344–347.
28. Zosimus, V, 26. Cf. Baynes, "Note on Bury's 'History,'" pp. 217–220, concerning chronology.
29. Claudian, De Con. Hon. IV, ll. 485ff: "in Latios ritus transistis Alani."

still on the steppes of south Russia living the wandering life of nomads.

The settling of Alans in Italy as military colonists by Stilicho or perhaps even earlier by Theodosius I was consistent with long-standing imperial policy. Such colonists were given lands from the imperial fisc and in return they were obligated to provide troops for the army. A high-ranking regiment of the Roman army stationed in Italy at this time was the *Comites Alani*. An Alan regiment continued to serve in northern Italy until at least 487, at which time it was stationed at Ravenna.[30]

The Alans serving in Rome's military forces had an important effect on the general level of competence of the imperial cavalry. Vegetius indicates that the example set by the Goths, the Alans, and the Huns led to the improvement of the imperial cavalry, but also, unfortunately, to the neglect of the infantry. Moreover, Gratian, perhaps because he first recruited Alans for the Roman army, was blamed for precipitating the decline of the infantry, the erstwhile backbone of the imperial military. By the end of the fourth century, Roman officers (if the observations of Vegetius can be assumed to represent this group) regarded the imperial cavalry as being of excellent quality and in no need of further improvement. These equestrian skills, which were brought to such a high level with the help of Alans and other steppe peoples, soon found their way into panegyric. Vegetius could devise no more flattering way to characterize the emperor's ability as a horseman than to compare his prowess to that of the Alans and the Huns.[31]

Contemporary reports mentioning the Alans' assimilation into the Roman culture of Italy provide evidence of Alan service in imperial military units and of the influence they had on the training and development of Roman cavalry. Yet the *Notitia Dignitatum*, wherein one would expect to find included on the

30. On these military colonists in general, see A. H. M. Jones, *The Later Roman Empire*, I (Norman, Okla., 1964), 620. *Notitia Dignitatum, oc.*, VI, 50, VII, 163: "Comites Alani," and *Origo gentis Langobardorum*, ch. 3.
31. Vegetius, *Ep. rei milit.*, I, 20; III, 26. J. W. Eadie, "The Development of Roman Mailed Cavalry," *JRS*, LVII (1967), 161–173, deals with heavy cavalry, not Alan light cavalry.

lists of military colonies in Italy some reference to the settlements which were providing the Alan forces for Stilicho's armies, designates all such installations only by the uniform and uninformative term *Sarmatian*.[32] However, the information on the Alans in Italy offered above leads one to suspect that the term *Sarmatian* as used to describe all military settlements under consideration is not an accurate designation. A contemporary edict that found its way into the *Theodosian Code* confirms this suspicion. There one finds explicit mention of *Alamanni* as military colonists in Italy.[33] The question whether this mention of *Alamanni* is a simple miscasting of *Alani* (something which is not uncommon in both classical and early medieval sources)[34] or a true reading is not as essential as the doubt which the evidence from this edict casts upon the accuracy of the term *Sarmatian* as the exclusive modifier of the *laeti* listed in the Italian section of the *Notitia*. In this context it should be pointed out that the Alan chief Saul is called *praefectus* by a contemporary — the same title which was held by the commander of a *laeti* colony.[35]

Any attempt, however, to ascertain which of the colonies listed in the *Notitia* as Sarmatian were really inhabited by Alans can at best be a matter of informed conjecture. Let us begin by noting that many of the truly Sarmatian colonies in Italy, if indeed not all of them, had very probably been founded during the reign of Constantine the Great early in the fourth century.[36] In the three-quarters of a century or more which elapsed between the founding of these colonies and the drawing up of the part of the *Notitia* under discussion, some of the settlements within the original colonies may have ceased to function adequately; thus, we may infer that Alans were settled where Sarmatians had once

32. *Notitia Dignitatum, oc.*, XLII, 46–63.
33. *CTh*, VII, xx, 12, 400: "quisquis igitur laetus Alamannus Sarmata vagus vel filius veterani aut cuislibet corporis dilectui obnoxius et florentissimis legionibus inserendus." See Jones, *Later Roman Empire*, I, 620.
34. See, for example, Gregory, *Hist.*, II, 9, 19.
35. Claudian, *De Bel. Goth.*, ll. 581ff: "ibat patiens dicionis Alanus,/ qua nostrae iussere tubae, mortemque petendam/ pro Latio docuit gentis praefectus Alanae. . . ."
36. Albert Grenier, *Manuel d'archéologie Gallo-romaine*, V (Paris, 1931), 398ff. *CTh*, VII, 20, 12.

been or even in places where some of the latter still dwelt.[37] The great similarity of Alan and Sarmatian culture, including language, as well as the Alan's well-known assimilative propensities would probably have made such mixed settlements possible and perhaps even desirable. Therefore, it may be suggested that, since Alans were only being used to "fill in" existing Sarmatian installations, the bureaucrats who were in charge of *Notitia* simply saw no reason to alter the titular designations which had been used for almost a century, if not longer. We know that bureaucrats in general are conservative and we know in particular that those who were in charge of the *Notitia* were very conservative.[38]

In continuing this line of argument, we should note that of the three major battles in which Stilicho's Italian-based Alan troops played a significant role two were located at these military colonies. Pollentia, where the Alans were so eager to raise the siege that they attacked the Goths on Good Friday (thus alienating their Christian comrades) and where the over-zealousness of the Alan commander enabled Alaric to escape, was only twenty-five miles south of the colony at Turin. Verona, where the Alans fought bravely and their commander, the Prefect Saul, gave his life even after his loyalty to the empire had been impugned, was the headquarters of another colony.[39] Is it too extreme to suggest that the families of the Alan fighting men who served in such a distinguished manner at Pollentia and Verona may have been dwelling within the walls of these very cities? The Alan troops who served Stilicho in 405 were called upon to defend northern Italy against a large horde of barbari-

37. The terms *colony* and *settlement* are used here in a very specific sense. Colony refers to a military establishment of barbarians. Settlement refers to the physical location of the homes and other installations within a colony. Colony is an administrative designation and a particular colony might be made up of several settlements. See Grenier, *Manuel d'archéologie*, V, 397–402, and Bachrach, "Alans in Gaul," p. 478.

38. Jones, *Later Roman Empire*, II, 1417–1450, and J. B. Bury, "The Notitia Dignitatum," *JRS*, X (1920), 131–154.

39. *Notitia Dignitatum, oc.,* XLII, 63: "Praefectus Sarmatarum gentilium (in Liguria), Pollentia"; and 54: "Praefectus Sarmatarum gentilium [Veronae]."

ans; all the colonies under discussion were located in northern Italy.

At least two other cities in northern Italy which were the headquarters of military colonies or very close to such headquarters were the scenes of military activity involving the Alans during the second half of the fifth century. While on his way to subdue an Alan uprising, the Emperor Majorian was killed at the colony at Tortona. A few years later, Ricimer defeated an Alan force at Bergamo, a city in the midst of several colonies and settlements, notably, Novara, Sarmarate, and Verona.[40]

The Sarmatian military colonies under consideration were strategically placed throughout northern Italy and protected many of the major roads leading to the Alpine passes from north to south and roads across the peninsula from east to west. Interspersed among the headquarter cities of these military colonies were a considerable number of places with names that suggest Alan settlement or influence. About five miles north of Aosta along the road leading out of the St. Bernard Pass to the Sarmatian settlement of Ivrea is the town of Allain. This town is thirty miles to the east of Alagna, a strategically located settlement which has always been a center of military importance. To the south, some three miles northwest of the colony at Vercelli, is another place called Alagna. To the southeast of Vercelli on the road to Pavia in the broad plain of the Po is the town of Alagna Lomellina. Between the headquarters at Tortona and Cremona, only about ten miles north of Sarmato, is a town called in the medieval documents Alan d'Riano (modern Landriano). Further to the north and east on the road from the Brenner Pass to the colony at Verona is the town of Allegno, and to the east along the road leading from the Alps to the colony headquarters at Oderza is Alano di Piave (see map 2).[41]

40. *Ibid.*, 57, Tortona; 58, Novara; 54, Verona. For Sarmarate, see *Dizionario Enciclopedico dei comuni d'Italia*, I.2 (Rome, 1950), 406, and Dante Olivieri, *Dizionario di Toponomastica Lombarda*, 2nd ed. (Milan, 1961), p. 17. For the activities of Majorian and Ricimer, see Jordanes, *Getica*, XLV.

41. For the Sarmatian colonies, see *Notitia Dignitatum, oc.*, XLII, 62, Ivrea; 59, Vercelli; 54, Verona; 52, Oderza. For the Alan place names, see appendix III, nos. 29, 2, 3, 4, 50, 41, 23, respectively.

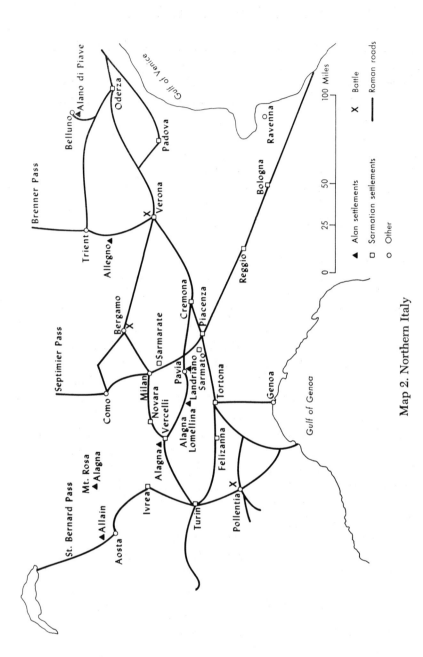

Map 2. Northern Italy

40

THE ALANS COME TO THE WEST

All the evidence suggests that the term *Sarmatian* as used to describe the imperial military colonies in northern Italy is not completely accurate, and that by the early fifth century the usage "Alano-Sarmatian" would have been more representative of the true state of affairs. Since a noteworthy number of Alan place names have survived into modern times, perhaps it can be assumed that the Lombard historian Paul the Deacon was using the word *Sarmatian* to mean Alans as well, when in the eighth century he indicated that place names of "Sarmatian" origin still survived in northern Italy.[42] In general it is reasonable to conclude that militarily significant Alan forces were settled in strategic positions throughout northern Italy in close proximity to the older settlements of their Sarmatian brethren.

ALANS AT CONSTANTINOPLE

When Theodosius I went west to deal with the usurper Eugenius in 392, he took with him the bulk of the eastern army. Arcadius, Theodosius's eldest son, was left to reign at Constantinople, but Rufinus, a Gallo-Roman noble of great ability, actually directed affairs in the East. With the eastern part of the empire all but devoid of troops, it was necessary for Rufinus to recruit barbarians to defend Constantinople. Among those barbarians who found the lure of Roman gold and a privileged position in the eastern part of the empire attractive were bands of Alans and Huns.[43]

In 395, Gainas, a Gothic general and a supporter of Stilicho, the military commander in the West, led many of the troops that Theodosius had taken from the East back again to Constantinople. Upon his arrival, Gainas had Rufinus murdered. Subsequently, a struggle for power developed between the German party led by Gainas and an anti-German party. In 400 the anti-German reaction reached its high point and Gainas, along with

42. Paul, *Hist.*, II, 26.
43. Claudian, *Contra Ruf.*, I, ll. 308ff; II, ll. 268ff. Demougeot, *L'empire romain*, pp. 155–158.

many of his Gothic followers, was murdered. For the next two decades Romans dominated affairs at Constantinople.[44]

Support for the anti-German party came from a band of Huns led by Uldis, who together with a force of Alans had earlier served under Rufinus. Although Uldis's Huns later turned their interest away from imperial service, some of the Alans remained loyal to the government at Constantinople. By 421 at least one Alan, a certain Ardaburius, had risen to the high rank of general in the East Roman army. In that year he led a force against the Persians in Arzanene and defeated them. He followed up that victory by successfully besieging the fortified city of Nisibis.[45]

Three years later Ardaburius commanded an East Roman force which invaded Italy for the purpose of overthrowing the usurper John and placing Valentinian III on the throne. Ardaburius's son Aspar served as his second in command and led the cavalry. After some initial setbacks, the eastern force was successful; as a reward for effectively carrying out this difficult campaign, Ardaburius was made consul for the year 427.[46] Although Ardaburius continued to hold high military commands at Constantinople until at least 442, Aspar emerged as the dominant military figure in the East Roman empire. In 431 Aspar commanded a large army which was sent against the Vandals in Africa. The approach of this force seems to have made it necessary for Gaiseric, the king of the Vandals and Alans who had recently invaded North Africa, to abandon temporarily the siege of Hippo which he had been carrying on since his arrival. In any event, Aspar led his forces against Gaiseric, and in an open battle the barbarians won a decisive victory over the East Roman army.

44. Thompson, *Attila and the Huns*, pp. 32, 54, 58, and Demougeot, *L'empire romain*, pp. 256–261.

45. Demougeot, *L'empire romain*, pp. 256–261, and Bury, *History of the Later Roman Empire*, II (New York, 1958), 4. Ernst Stein, *Histoire du bas-empire*, I (Paris, 1959), 281, and Jones, *Later Roman Empire*, I, 181. Priscus, *fr.* 20; Evagrius, II, 1; and Socrates, VII, 18.

46. Bury, *Later Roman Empire*, I, 222–225; Stein, *Bas-empire*, I, 282–285; and S. I. Oost, *Galla Placidia Augusta* (Chicago, 1968), pp. 183, 188–189. Olymp., *fr.* 46; Socrates, VII, 23; John of Ant., *fr.* 175; Procopius, *B.V.*, I, iii, 8; and Philostorgius, XII, 11. A. Demandt, "Magister militum," *RE*, suppl. XII (1970), cols. 746–781, gathers the material on Aspar and his family (with charts).

Aspar then spent the next three years in Africa where he negotiated a treaty between the empire and Gaiseric. This treaty seems to have been very important, and, although it was not officially made public until 435, Valentinian, the ruler in the West, made Aspar consul for the year 434, presumably as a reward for the role he played in bringing about the forthcoming treaty. A beautiful silver disc depicting Aspar and his family and celebrating the consulship survives today (see plate 1).[47]

Through the later 430s and 440s Aspar dominated the East Roman military. When Carthage fell to Gaiseric in 439, Theodosius II responded by sending a huge fleet and invasion force into the West. The commanders, who were Aspar's friends and relatives, never attacked the Vandal homeland and were content to spend the years 440–442 in and around Sicily accomplishing nothing. These forces were recalled in the latter year to deal with Hunnic attacks on the eastern frontier. Aspar, however, negotiated a treaty before the campaigning season of 442 began, and the Huns did not bother the eastern part of the empire in that year. In 443 Aspar's troops, which had been in the West under

47. Bury, *Later Roman Empire*, I, 225, 247–248; Stein *Bas-empire*, I, 321; Oost, *Galla Placidia*, p. 228; and Jones, *Later Roman Empire*, I, 181. Procopius, *B.V.*, I, iii, 33ff. On the disc, see W. Meyer, "Zwei antike Elfenbeintafel der königlisch Staats-Bibliothek in München," *Abhandlungen der Königlisch-Bayerischen Akademie der Wissenschaften*, XV (1879), 6–7, and R. Delbrueck, *Die Consular Diptychen und verwandte Denkmäler* (Berlin and Leipzig, 1929), pp. 154–155, and pl. 35. See also Ludwig Schmidt, *Geschichte der Wandalen* (Munich, 1942), pp. 63ff.

Although Aspar probably returned to Constantinople in 435 and thus was not present at the formalization of the treaty between Gaiseric and the West Roman government, his absence at this final stage of events is hardly evidence that he was not responsible for negotiating the agreement or at least for having established the groundwork for it. Aspar was the most prominent imperial personage in North Africa during the period before the signing of the treaty, i.e., during the negotiations, and in 434 before he returned to Constantinople he was given an extremely high honor by the West Roman emperor. Aspar surely was not rewarded with this consulship for having been defeated by the Vandals several years earlier or for having accomplished nothing of value to the West Roman government. If Aspar did not lay the groundwork for the treaty with Gaiseric, then who did? If Aspar was not made consul for the service of negotiating the treaty, then why was he made consul? Those who would discount Aspar's role in these events must provide more convincing answers to the questions above. (See below for further evidence of Aspar's positive relations with Gaiseric.)

Ariobindus and the other generals, finally returned and went to war against the Huns. Aspar's armies were defeated on a number of occasions by the Huns and met a final disaster in the Chersonesus, which according to a contemporary, Priscus, all but destroyed the last Roman field army in the East.[48]

Despite these disasters, Aspar still remained the dominant force in East Roman politics. In 447 Aspar's eldest son Ardaburius, who was named for his grandfather, was made consul. In 450, when the Emperor Theodosius II died, substantial support was generated for Aspar to take the imperial throne offered to him by the senate of Constantinople. A later contemporary quotes Aspar, who refused the offer, to the effect that by becoming emperor he would set a precedent which would not be healthy for the empire. Needless to say, such a precedent had been set almost two centuries earlier when Maximinus became the first barbarian general to assume the imperial purple. Incidentally, he too was an Alan. Whatever Aspar's real reasons might have been for declining the throne, he was intent upon exercising power. Thus he elevated his *domesticus* Marcian to the imperial throne. Marcian immediately showed his good faith and gratitude by appointing Ardaburius master of the soldiers in the East. Shortly after this, Marcian made Ardaburius a patrician.[49]

A curious story about Marcian told by the Byzantine historian Procopius suggests that there may have been some kind of informal agreement between Aspar and Gaiseric. When Aspar's army was defeated by Gaiseric in 431, Marcian, who was serving as a member of Aspar's staff, was captured by Gaiseric's forces. According to Procopius's account, Marcian was saved

48. Cf. E. A. Thompson, "The Foreign Policies of Theodosius II and Marcian," *Hermathena*, LXXV (1950), 63–66, and *Attila and the Huns*, pp. 78–85. For the names of the commanders, Theophanes, *Chron.* A.M. 5942 (wrong date). For the relationships Demandt, "Magister militum," chart. Cf. E. A. Thompson, "The Isaurians under Theodosius II," *Hermathena*, LXVIII (1946), 18–31, who argues that the Isaurians exercised considerable influence at Constantinople in the later 440s.

49. Thompson, *Attila and the Huns*, pp. 125ff; Bachrach, "Alans in Gaul," p. 481; Jones, *Later Roman Empire*, I, 218, 327. John Malalas, *fr.* XIV; Marcellinus Comes, *Chron.*, 471; and Priscus, *fr.* 20. See also Zonaras, XIV, 1, for the problems of Arians in power.

from execution when an eagle flying overhead cast a shadow over him. Gaiseric, who supposedly saw this phenomenon, interpreted it as a sign that Marcian would one day rule and thus he spared his life.[50]

Evagrius, a contemporary of Procopius, provides a slightly different version of this story—a version which he probably found in the *History* of Priscus. Evagrius writes:

> Another circumstance also occurred, which might serve as a prognostic of the imperial power being destined to Marcian. When serving against the Vandals, he was one of many who fell into their hands . . . and, on the demand of Genseric to see the prisoners, was dragged with the rest along the plain. . . . Genseric sat in an upper chamber, surveying with delight the numbers that had been taken. . . . Marcian laid himself down upon the ground to sleep in the sun, which was shining with unusual heat for the season of the year. An eagle, however, poising his flight above him, and directly intercepting the sun as with a cloud, thus produced a shade and its consequent refreshment, to the amazement of Genseric, who rightly presaging the future, sent for Marcian, and liberated him, having previously bound him by solemn oaths, that on attaining the imperial power he would maintain faithfully the rights of treaty towards the Vandals, and not commence hostilities against them; and Procopius records that Marcian observed these conditions.[51]

Scholars agree that this tale was semi-official propaganda used by the East Roman government to explain its failure to take military action against the Vandals who finally sacked Rome in 455 without the East doing anything to stop them or retaliate.[52] Within this context, it should be remembered that Marcian was Aspar's handpicked candidate for emperor, and it is difficult to imagine that this hands-off policy regarding the Vandals and Alans in North Africa was formulated by anyone other than the Alan general-in-chief.

50. Procopius, *B.V.*, I, iv, iff. See the discussion by T. Hodgkin, *Italy and Her Invaders*, 2nd ed. (Oxford, 1892), II, 261–262.

51. Evagrius, II, 1. The translation is from *Ecclesiastical History* (London, 1846), pp. 44–45.

52. Thompson, "Foreign Policies," pp. 66–69; E. F. Gautier, *Genséric Roi des Vandales* (Paris, 1935), pp. 239–240; E. Kaegi, *Byzantium and the Decline of Rome* (Princeton, 1968), pp. 29–30; Stein, *Bas-empire*, I, 358. Procopius, *B.V.*, I, iv, iff.

The suggestion that Aspar and Gaiseric made some kind of personal arrangement back in 431 is supported not only by affairs during Marcian's reign, but by earlier evidence as well. During Aspar's stay in Africa (431–434), he maintained cordial relations with Gaiseric; they exchanged gifts and negotiated a treaty which, as has been mentioned, earned the former the consulship with its attendant prestige and influence. In 440 when Theodosius II sent a fleet to take back Carthage which Gaiseric had recently captured, Aspar's commanders never attacked but kept their men idle in Sicily for more than two years. When Marcian died in 457 and Leo, another of Aspar's choices, was made emperor, African-East Roman relations remained peaceful despite the efforts of Majorian, the West Roman emperor, to interest Leo in his venture to conquer the Vandals and the Alans.[53]

In these early years Aspar seems to have controlled Leo fairly well. Leo promised to give his daughter Leontia in marriage to Aspar's son Patricius and to elevate his future son-in-law to the rank of Caesar, thus placing him in line to become emperor. Leo also seems to have made Aspar's youngest son, Hermaneric, consul. Leo's subservience to Aspar, however, did not content him. He put off the wedding of Leontia and Patricius and married his other daughter to an Isaurian officer who took the name of Zeno. With the support of Zeno and his Isaurian forces, Leo slowly began to assert his independence from Aspar. Among the disagreements they had was one over who should be sent as an envoy to Gaiseric. Against Aspar's advice, Leo sent his trusted supporter Tatianus. Gaiseric, however, refused to deal in a positive manner with Tatianus, who returned home to report his failure to gain the king's acquiescence to Leo's plans. East Roman relations with Africa continued to decline during the 460s in rough coincidence with Leo's attempts to act independently of Aspar and to interfere with Gaiseric's policies in the western Mediterranean. Finally, in 467 a rumor spread through the East that Gaiseric was planning an invasion of Alexandria. It may be

53. Kaegi, *Byzantium*, pp. 29–30, and the sources cited in n. 66.

suggested that the Vandal attacks noted by Procopius (but not dated), which were directed against Illyria and parts of Greece, were a prelude to a threatened assault on Alexandria.[54]

Leo, however, seems to have been willing to gamble that he could ultimately free himself from Aspar and destroy the Vandal and Alan kingdom in Africa in one bold stroke. He expended huge sums of gold and silver to procure a fleet and an invasion force. He was very careful, in addition, not to give command of this operation to Aspar or to any of his sons. In describing these events, Procopius indicates that Aspar made many attempts to have the idea of invasion abandoned and that he knew Leo's independence would be firmly established if his troops could defeat the Vandals and Alans in Africa. It seems, however, that Aspar's influence on Basilicus, the commander of the expedition, helped to bring about a barbarian victory, a conclusion which benefited the Alan cause both in Africa and at Constantinople.[55]

The evidence may not be sufficient for us to conclude with certainty that Gaiseric and Aspar had made some kind of informal personal arrangement in 431–432 by which Aspar promised to keep the East Roman government from interfering with the barbarians in North Africa and by which Gaiseric promised to do all in his power to support Aspar's dominant position at Constantinople. Whether or not there was such an arrangement, events worked out as though there had been one. It would only be conjecture to say that this apparent community of interest between the Alan general and the king of the Alans and Vandals

54. Bury, *Later Roman Empire*, I, 317, and E. W. Brooks, "The Emperor Zenon and the Isaurians," *EHR*, XXX (1893), 211–212. See also Evagrius, III, 26, where he quotes Eustathius. On the projected attack on Alexandria, *V. Dan.*, ch. 65. Jones, *Later Roman Empire*, I, 222, notes that the rumor that the Vandals would attack Alexandria came soon after the announcement that Zeno would marry Leo's daughter Ariadne. On Tatianus, see Jones, *Later Roman Empire*, p. 221, Candidus, *fr.* 1, and Priscus, *fr.* 35. On the other raids, Procopius, *B.V.*, I, v, 23.

55. Brooks, "Zenon and the Isaurians," pp. 213–215; Bury, *Later Roman Empire*, I, 317–319; Stein, *Bas-empire*, I, 358–360; Courtois, *Les Vandales*, pp. 201–202; Kaegi, *Byzantium*, pp. 35ff. Procopius, *B.V.*, I, vi, iff; Priscus, *fr.* 42; Candidus, *fr.* 2; Theophanes, *Chron.* A.M. 5963. Cf. G. M. Bersanetti, "Basilisco e l'imperatore Leone I," *Rendiconti della Pontifica Accademia di Archeologia*, XX (1943–1944), 331–346, who argues against collusion.

had an ethnic basis. On this point, Professor Gautier has concluded, perhaps somewhat too boldly: "Pour nier que, à la base de cette neutralité et de ces relations anciennes, il ait pu y avoir une sympathie ethnique, une complicité de clan, entre les Alains de Constantinople et ceux de Carthage, il faudrait être convaincu *a priori* que le titre *Rex Alanorum* était simplement protocolaire."[56] In a history of the Alans such an inference is indeed attractive.

The Vandal-Alan victory over Leo's forces in 468 marked an upturn in the fortunes of Aspar's house. Leo permitted Aspar's son to marry his daughter and raised him to the rank of Caesar. As a Caesar, Patricius entered what may be considered the legitimate line of succession to the imperial throne. Shortly afterward, opposition to Patricius's elevation to this new position led to street riots and other popular outbreaks by those who seemingly rejected the idea that an Arian might become emperor. Thus the orthodox population of Constantinople, led by the clergy and perhaps encouraged by Leo's agents, weakened the position of Aspar and his family once again.[57]

To this setback was added the exposure of several plots hatched by Ardaburius, Aspar's eldest son. Ardaburius tried unsuccessfully to gain through bribery the support of some of Zeno's Isaurian followers. These efforts were reported to Leo as were Ardaburius's communications with Anagast, a general stationed in Thrace, in an attempt to obtain his support for a revolt. The most damaging of Ardaburius's intrigues involved his dealings with the Persians. His endeavors to obtain Persian support against Leo were exposed in the senate when the emperor produced letters from Ardaburius to the Persians which outlined his plot. Aspar, who was at the senate that day, could find no way to defend his son and was forced to disown him publicly.[58]

56. Gautier, *Genséric*, p. 240.
57. Brooks, "Zenon and the Isaurians," p. 214; Bury, *Later Roman Empire*, I, 319; Zonaras, XIV, 1; and Victor Tonn., *an.* 470. It is dangerous to take at face value the sources' emphasis on religion. These writers were usually clerics and tended to see events in a biased manner.
58. Stein, *Bas-empire*, I, 360–361; Jones, *Later Roman Empire*, I, 222–223. Candidus, *fr.* 1; John of Ant., *fr.* 206; Priscus, *fr.* 20.

Whether Ardaburius had taken the initiative in these conspiracies which brought about his disgrace or whether he was merely acting under his father's orders cannot be ascertained. The latter supposition seems more probable. In the wake of these events Leo acted decisively. In a swift move which earned him the sobriquet "butcher," Leo had Aspar and Ardaburius murdered in the palace by some eunuchs. Patricius, whose assassination was also attempted, managed to escape though he was severely wounded. Hermaneric, Aspar's youngest son, about whom very little is known, was not at the palace when the assassinations took place and seems to have survived.[59]

For almost a half century these Alans were prominent and frequently dominant at Constantinople. They maintained their positions, in part, because they were very able men and proved it by leading their forces to victory or by providing other useful services to the empire. Another reason for their success is that, even though they were barbarians, they were not Germans and thus they escaped the East Romans' anti-German purge during the early fifth century. When during the last years of the fourth century the Goths swore not to serve the empire and most of them did not break their oath, Rufinus recruited Alans and Huns to serve at Constantinople. When the few Goths and other Teutons who did serve the empire in the East were the object of a bloody anti-German reaction, it was the Huns and the Alans who helped the Romans succeed. At Constantinople, in the wake of the massacre of Gainas and his German followers, the Alan Ardaburius and his son Aspar emerged as generals of consequence.

Personal ability and political conditions did not account completely for Alan power at Constantinople. Aspar and his family had substantial numbers of Alans settled around the Black Sea upon whom they could call for military support. In the eastern part of the Crimea, for example, Alans were settled for many years. An early medieval geographer, writing in Greek, points out that the Alans renamed the former Greek city of Theodosia

59. Jones, *Later Roman Empire*, I, 223. Marcellinus Comes, *Chron.*, 471; Candidus, *fr.* 1; Procopius, *B.V.*, I, vi, 27.

A History of the Alans

in their own language, calling it Ardabda.[60] Alans also lived along the western shore of the Black Sea in lower Moesia and Scythia minor. These settlements probably were established in the late fourth or early fifth centuries. The Alans dwelling in this region were recognized as federates by the Emperor Marcian. Candac, the Alan ruler in this area, was a supporter of Aspar, the puppeteer who pulled Marcian's strings.[61]

Once Aspar and his family had secured their position and had taken full advantage of their Alan and non-Germanic heritage, they did not hesitate to arrange marriage alliances with families of Germanic leaders who controlled substantial military forces. Intermarriage with Romans was also encouraged. Aspar had three wives and three sons; Ardaburius, the eldest, bore an Alan name, Patricius, the middle one, was given a Roman name, and Hermaneric, the youngest, had a German name. It may be conjectured that of Aspar's three wives the first one was an Alan, the second a Roman, and the third a German, thus explaining the sons' names. If this were the case, then Patricius was indeed the son best suited to marry the emperor's daughter since he was at least half-Roman. Intermarriage could be profitable and it almost led to an Alan becoming emperor. On a lower level we learn that Candac acquired valuable Ostrogothic connections by arranging marriage alliances with important Germans. If the interchange of Gothic and Alan names may be used as an additional measure of ethnic mixing, then Aspar's son Hermaneric with a German name can be compared with the

60. Alexandre Baschmakoff, *La synthèse des périplus pontiques* (Paris, 1948), p. 146; Aubrey Diller, *The Tradition of the Minor Greek Geographers*, in *Monographs of the American Philosophical Association*, XIV (1952), 133. See also R. Uhden, "Bemerkungen zu dem römischen Kartenfragment von Dura Europos," *Hermes*, LXVII (1932), 119; A. A. Vasiliev, *The Goths in Crimea* (Cambridge, Mass., 1936), p. 147. On the spelling of Ardabda, cf. Müllenhoff, *Deutsche Altertumskunde*, III, 114, who prefers Abdarda; and on the date, cf. Diller, *Tradition of the Minor Greek Philosophers*, p. 113, who prefers the later sixth century for the *Periplus*, or about a century later than the traditionally accepted date. The cosmographer of Ravenna, IV, 2, who compiled his work about 475–480, notes the importance of the Alans in the Crimea.

61. Jordanes, *Getica*, L. The Alans so dominated this region that the Pruth River was at one time called the *Alanus* River. See Isidore, *Orig.*, IX, 2, 94. George Vernadsky, *Ancient Russia* (New Haven, 1943), p. 133.

Ostrogoth Andac who had an Alan name and an Alan wife, the sister of Candac.[62]

With the fall of Aspar's family at Constantinople, an important episode of Alan history in the eastern Roman empire is drawn to a close. This is not to say, however, that Alans did not play a role in the emerging Byzantine world which followed. On the contrary, the history of the Alans in south Russia and central Asia during the Middle Ages is worthy of close examination, although such is beyond the scope of the present work.

ALANS AND VANDALS

Among those groups of Alans which escaped Hunnish domination in the 370s and fled west, some allied with the Vandals who were settled in Pannonia. After not too many years, probably by the early 390s, the area in which these Alans and Vandals were dwelling no longer could provide sustenance adequate for their needs. Thus a large number of Alans and many of the Vandals began moving westward in search of greener pastures. Any move eastward by these Vandals and Alans had been precluded by the various groups of Goths, Huns, and Alans who themselves were pushing westward in need of more land, thus exerting some pressure on those dwelling in Pannonia to move still further west.[63]

This westward migration by the Alans and Vandals did not escape the notice of Stilicho, the Roman commander in the West. Stilicho, who himself was part Vandal, had a number of loyal Alans serving under his command in Italy; therefore, he did not hesitate to invite the Alans and Vandals who were fleeing from Pannonia to settle in Noricum and Raetia as Roman allies. Unfortunately, he was unable to make satisfactory arrangements with these newcomers, and in the winter of 401 they began plundering the provinces which it was hoped they would defend.

62. Jordanes, *Getica*, L, for Candac; Candidus, *fr.* 1. For further discussion of the family relationships, see Jones, *Later Roman Empire*, II, 1104–1105. Jones insists upon calling Aspar a German. Demandt, "Magister militum," chart, for further Gothic connections.

63. Jordanes, *Getica*, XXXI, XXII; Procopius, *B.V.*, I, iii, 1. Cf. Courtois, *Les Vandales*, pp. 38–39, and Demougeot, *L'empire romain*, p. 130.

In any event, Stilicho moved across the Alps and put an end to their depredations. Having been defeated, the Alans and Vandals apparently moved northward and east into Germany beyond the Rhine frontier[64] and outside the empire.[65]

We next hear of these groups some five years later when on December 31, 406, they led their mounts across the frozen Rhine and once again entered imperial territory.[66] One group of Vandals under its king, Godegisel, engaged Rome's Frankish allies in battle, and he was killed. His followers were in danger of being annihilated when a force of Alans, probably those led by

64. On the invasion of Raetia and Noricum and Stilicho's victory, see Demougeot, *L'empire romain*, pp. 268, n. 191, 355, 403, and Courtois, *Les Vandales*, p. 40. Marcellinus Comes, *Chron.*, 408; Orosius, *Hist.*, VII, 38.

65. The problem of identifying Alan artifacts in the area of west-central Europe from Pannonia to the north and west has yet to be solved. In part this inability to draw firm conclusions about such artifacts seems to be the result of the thorough manner in which the peoples of south Russia and central Asia influenced each other by adopting and adapting styles in art and armament to the point where the characteristics of different groups have become indistinguishable. Nevertheless, various attempts have been made to isolate particular motifs in the art of the peoples who crossed this area of west-central Europe, but none of these studies seem to have been notably successful. See Eduard Beninger, "Der westgotisch-alanische Zug nach Mitteleuropa," *Mannus Bibliothek*, LI (1931), 76ff; E. Polaschek, "Wiener Grabfunde aus der Zeit des untergehenden römischen Limes," *Wiener Prähistorisch Zeitschrift*, XIX (1932), 239–258; A. Alföldi, "Funde aus der Hunnenzeit un ihre ethniche Sonderung," *Archaeologica Hungarica*, IX (Budapest, 1932); Otto Maenchen-Helfen, "Huns and Hsiung-Nu," *Byzantion*, XVII (1944–1945), 239–241; Thompson, *Attila and the Huns*, pp. 4–6; Werner, *Attila-Reiches*, pp. 15ff; Sulimirski, *The Sarmatians*, pp. 183ff; and V. A. Kuznetsov and V. K. Pudovin, "Alany v Zapadnoi Europe v epokhu 'Velikogo pereseleniia narodov,'" *Sovetskaia Arkheologiia*, II (1961), 79–85. Cf. Orosius, *Hist.*, I, 2, on *Alania*.

66. *Chron. Gall.*, ch. 63; Jordanes, *Getica*, XXXI; Prosp., *Epit. Chron.*, ch. 1230; Gregory, *Hist.*, II, 10; Zosimus, VI, 3, 1; Orosius, *Hist.*, VII, 38, 40; and Hydatius, *Chron.*, ch. 42. While the union of Alans and Vandals for the invasion of 406 is generally accepted by scholars, there is some doubt whether the Sueves played a role in these events. Most scholars argue that the Sueves were not joined with the Alans and Vandals during the crossing of the Rhine but united with them later for the invasion of Spain. Robert Reynolds, "Reconsideration of the History of the Suevi," *RBPH*, XXXV (1957) 19–47, argues that the Suevi were not associated with the Alans and the Vandals but came to Spain by sea. He suggests a relationship between the Sueves who went to Spain and the Swaefs who settled in England. Cf. Demougeot, *L'empire romain*, pp. 382ff, and Courtois, *Les Vandales*, pp. 38ff.

Respendial, came to their aid, attacked the Franks, defeated them, and saved the remaining Vandals.[67]

Two choices generally faced barbarians who had successfully entered imperial territory: inclusion within the Roman system as allies or a roving life of raiding and plunder. Though settlement and alliance did not seem to have been attractive to the Alans and Vandals in Raetia and Noricum about 400, Roman officials in Gaul nevertheless opened negotiations with the invaders. Thus while Respendial and Godegisel were fighting against the Franks, Goar, another Alan leader, was coming to terms with the empire.[68]

As Goar's followers were being settled in strategic positions, the Alans and Vandals who did not accept imperial hospitality began plundering throughout Gaul from Tournai in the north to Beziers in the south. Some two dozen cities and towns are cited in the sources as having been attacked by the invaders: Thérouanne, Arras, Tournai, Amiens, Laon, Rheims, Mayence, Worms, Spire, Strasbourg, Toulouse, Metz, Langres, Arcis-sur-Aube, Besançon, Autun, Clermont-Ferrand, Uzès, Arles, Béziers, Eauze, Bazas, Angoulême, and Meung-sur-Loire. The bulk of this evidence is, however, of dubious value, and any attempt to reconstruct the itinerary of the invaders' activities is little more than wishful thinking. Yet, even if only half of the many references to these attacks are accurate, it seems reasonable to assume that the Alans and Vandals divided into several, if not many, groups. The sources usually mention the Vandals and occasionally the Vandals and Alans together, but there are no mentions of independent groups of Alans in this episode. This would seem to sug-

67. Gregory, *Hist.*, II, 9: "Renatus Profuturus Frigiretus, cui iam supra meminimus, cum Roman refert a Gothic captam atque subversam, ait: 'Interea Respendial rex Alanorum, Goare ad Romanos transgresso, de Reno agmen suorum convertit, Wandalis Francorum bello laborantibus, Godigyselo rege absumpto, aciae viginti ferme milibus ferro preemptis, cunctis Wandalorum ad internitionem delendis, nisi Alanorum vis in tempore subvenisset.'" The manuscript tradition is confused on whether Alans or Alamans are meant, and scholars are in overwhelming agreement upon the former as the correct reading. See Courtois, *Les Vandales*, pp. 41–42.

68. Gregory, *Hist.*, II, 9.

gest that divisions were not made along tribal lines in the organization of these raiding parties.[69]

No evidence survives indicating that the invaders met any resistance from the Gallo-Romans. Bishop Paulinus of Béziers scolded his flock for its failure to oppose the enemy. He points out that, while the Vandals burn and the Alans ride away with the booty they have seized, the people of Béziers (all of Gaul?) hurry to replant their vines and return to everyday life; the theater and astrology, he says, preoccupy their interest while patriotism and morality are sorely lacking. Paulinus contrasts the weaknesses of this materialistic attitude to the strengths of religious morality, which he asserts would provide an effective shield even against the Alans' assaults.[70]

It should be noted that, while the Alans and Vandals were ravaging Gaul, a considerable force of imperial troops was also stationed there. When Constantine III usurped power in Britain and landed in Gaul in 407, he brought with him much of the field army from Britain. He also had the support of the Frankish federates who had been defeated by Respendial's Alans as well as perhaps that of the *Alamanni* settled in the Rhineland. It seems impossible that no agreement was reached between Constantine on the one hand and the leaders of the Alans and the Vandals on the other by which each group was enabled to pursue its own interests.[71] Gerontius, one of Constantine's generals, acquired a very loyal Alan bodyguard while in Gaul. This suggests at least

69. Courtois, *Les Vandales*, pp. 42–51, makes an exhaustive study of the evidence for this three-year occupation of Gaul. See also Schmidt, *Der Wandalen*, pp. 17–18, and Demougeot, *L'empire romain*, pp. 381–387. Specific information concerning what the Alan raiders did is nonexistent. We know that they entered Gaul, we know that they remained allied with the Vandals, and we know that they left Gaul and entered Spain together. The most important text concerning the cities sacked in Gaul by the Vandals and the Alans is St. Jerome, *Epist.* CXXIII, 16.

There is a tradition which survives in the accounts of Isidore of Seville (*Hist. Wand.*, ch. 71) and Orosius (*Hist.*, VII, 403) that the invaders tried to reach Spain as early as 407 but that they were turned back and only then did they plunder Gaul.

70. Paulinus of Béziers, *Epigramma*, ll. 18–29.

71. Demougeot, *L'empire romain*, pp. 382–395, provides a detailed account of Constantine III's activities. See also Courtois, *Les Vandales*, pp. 52–53.

some degree of close contact between Constantine's forces and the Alans.[72]

One may wonder just how many Alans joined Constantine's army. From among those barbarians who did join him, Constantine created a regiment called the *Honorians*. This force served directly under the command of Gerontius who conquered Spain. As a reward for their loyal service and in an unusual example of preferential treatment, Gerontius permitted the *Honorians* to plunder the plains of Palantia. Afterward he provided them with lands for settlement so that they would be in a position to hold the passes of the Pyrenees.[73] In 409, however, these *Honorians* allowed the Alans and Vandals to enter Spain without providing any opposition.[74] It may be conjectured that the *Honorians*, who are known to have been barbarians and who were given preferential treatment by Gerontius (a general who was well served by his Alan bodyguard), were Alans, and therefore they permitted their brethren to enter Spain. A search of the toponymical evidence in the passes of the Pyrenees produces the name Bréche d'Allanz. This is the only surviving place name which illustrates that perhaps at least some of the *Honorians* settled to defend the passes of the Pyrenees were Alans.[75]

When the Alans and Vandals entered Spain, they continued the raiding and plundering which had characterized their stay in Gaul. The Hispano-Romans, like their fellow citizens in Gaul, seem to have made no effort to engage the invaders in combat; rather, they simply shut themselves up in the fortified cities, towns, and castra in the hope that the Alans and the Vandals would disappear. The Alans and the Vandals who were horsemen seem to have made no attempt to besiege these positions. The inhabitants, though able to venture into the countryside only at some risk, found the fields stripped of edibles. In some areas the people were reduced to starvation, and contemporaries

72. Sozomen, IX, xiii, 4, and Olymp., *fr.* 16.
73. Orosius, *Hist.*, VII, 40, 7–10, and Sozomen, IX, xii, 7.
74. *Chron. Gall.*, ch. 552, II; Hydatius, *Chron.*, ch. 42; Isidore, *Hist. Wand.*, ch. 71. On this see Courtois, *Les Vandales*, p. 52, and Demougeot, *L'empire romain*, pp. 394–395.
75. See appendix II, no. 45, and map 1.

gossiped that it was not uncommon for a mother to eat her own children.[76]

After some two years of ravaging and raiding, the Alan and Vandal leaders made an arrangement with the Hispano-Romans for a division of the land. The Alans settled in Lusitania and Cartagena, the Siling Vandals in Baetica, and the Hasding Vandals in Gallaecia among the Sueves. These settlements seem to have been arranged on a hospitality basis, i.e., the Alans and other invaders became the guests of the Roman landowners and thus received a significant portion of the income from their estates. In return for this income, the guests "protected" their hosts from raiders and plunderers. These arrangements seem to have temporarily brought peace to Spain.[77]

The Alans and Vandals who settled in Spain hoped to be recognized as federates by the empire. They communicated this desire to the Emperor Honorius, asking for peace, promising to give hostages to ensure their loyalty, and offering to fight for the empire as allies. Constantius, the Roman commander in the West, chose rather to use the Visigoths, whom he had recently forced to submit, to subdue and weaken the Alans and Vandals in Spain. The Visigoths then attacked the Alans who were settled in Lusitania and the Siling Vandals who were in Baetica. According to the sources, after three years of warfare, the Visigoths wore down both enemies, almost annihilating them. The Siling Vandal King Fredbal was captured and Addoc, the Alan king in Lusitania, was killed. Guntharic, the Vandal king in Gallaecia, seems to have been accepted as an imperial ally. Not only was he not attacked by the Visigoths, but he appears to have led his forces against the Alans in Cartagena. There he reduced Respendial's followers to impotence. When these groups had been subdued, Guntharic dominated all the remaining Vandals and Alans in Spain. His position was protected by the

76. Hydatius, *Chron.*, chs. 46, 47, 48; Isidore, *Hist. Wand.*, ch. 72; Olymp. *fr.* 30. See also Courtois, *Les Vandales*, pp. 52–53.
77. Hydatius, *Chron.*, ch. 49; Isidore, *Hist. Wand.*, ch. 73. On the division of the land between Romans and barbarians, see F. Lot, "Hospitalité," pp. 975–1011. See also Courtois, *Les Vandales*, pp. 52–53.

Roman commander Constantius, who withdrew the Visigoths from Spain and settled them in southern Gaul. This last move also suggests that there was an agreement between the empire and Guntharic.[78]

The subsequent history of the remnants of Addoc's and Respendial's Alan followers cannot be separated from that of the Vandals led by Guntharic and his successors. Their remaining years in Spain, the invasion and conquest of North Africa, the sack of Rome, and their eventual defeat and destruction by Belisarius's armies are the highlights of a much more detailed and complex history which marked Vandal and Alan prominence in the western Mediterranean for more than a century. The story has been told in detail on several occasions, but the role played by the Alans has been neglected. The tendency has been to conclude that the Alans were completely assimilated by the politically dominant Vandal majority.[79] Contemporary accounts, however, indicate that the Alans remained an identifiable element within the total group which also included barbarians other than the Vandals. Bishop Possidius of Calma, who was at Hippo during the Alan and Vandal siege which lasted more than a year, clearly distinguishes between the Alans and the Vandals, adding that there were some Goths who took part as well. This distinction between Alans and Vandals is also noted by the poet Dracontius, who flourished in North Africa late in the fifth century. He was a poet at the court of the Vandal monarch Gunthamund, a man who was very easily offended. Thus, in a poem in which a list of barbarians are noted in a pejorative manner, Dracontius includes the Alans but omits the Vandals; this suggests that the Vandal king enjoyed hearing of the deprecation of the Alans. Procopius indicates clearly that both Alans and Vandals formed the fighting forces of the North African kingdom. He adds that

78. Orosius, *Hist.*, VII, 43, 14; Hydatius, *Chron.*, chs. 60, 68; Isidore, *Hist. Goth.*, chs. 22, 68; Isidore, *Hist. Wand.*, ch. 73; Sidonius Apollinaris, *Carm.*, II, ll. 363ff; *Chron. Gall.*, chs. 562, 564. See Courtois, *Les Vandales*, p. 54; Thompson, "Southern Gaul," p. 67; Bachrach, "Southern Gaul," pp. 355–357.

79. Schmidt, *Deutsche Stämme*, I, 49, considers the Alans "vollig germanisiert." Cf. Gautier, *Genséric*, pp. 83–84, 239–240.

the term *Vandal* is often used in a very general manner to denote all the non-Moorish barbarians in North Africa. The Emperor Justinian, whose armies ultimately destroyed the kingdom of the Vandals and Alans, officially recognized the existence of both peoples.[80]

Perhaps the most striking evidence of Alan importance among the Vandals was the retention by the king of the title *Rex Vandalorum et Alanorum*. After Guntharic assumed this title in about 419, each subsequent monarch down to the Roman reconquest of North Africa retained it. Had the Alans been assimilated by the Vandals, the need or even the desirability of keeping the dual title would be questionable. It would be a constant reminder to the Alans' descendants of their erstwhile independence. Conversely, only if the Alans did maintain a modicum of identity and independence would the dual basis of the royal title have political significance; this would be a sound reason for its survival.[81]

It may be further noted that in the military, where the Alans played an important role, mounted troops were the predominant element; the kings of the Vandals and Alans placed no faith in infantry. The rejection of foot soldiering, though not unique to the Alans, was shared traditionally by other nomad peoples of the steppes; the Germans, however, were not averse to this form of warfare.[82]

Whereas the Vandals apparently came to rely upon mounted combat through the influence of their Alan allies, the Alans, on the other hand, seem to have adopted the Arian Christianity of the former and thus abandoned or at least tempered their native religion.[83] Thus, although the Alans and the Vandals each main-

80. Possidius, *V. Aug.*, ch. 28; Dracontius, *Romulea*, V, ll. 33ff; Procopius, *B.V.*, I, v, 18; and Just., *Nov.*, xxx, xi, 2.
81. Vict. Vit., II, 39; III, 3; *CIL*, VIII, 13734. Gautier, *Genséric*, pp. 239–240.
82. Charles Oman, *A History of the Art of War in the Middle Ages*, I (London, 1924), 29–30; E. A. Thompson, *The Early Germans* (Oxford, 1965), pp. 123–124; Schmidt, *Der Wandalen*, p. 165, n. 4; Courtois, *Les Vandales*, p. 231, n. 8; and Bachrach, "Armorican Chivalry," pp. 167–168.
83. Bede, *Chron.*, ch. 480: "Effera gens Vandalorum, Halanorum et Gothorum ab Hispaniis ad Afracam transiens omnia ferro flamma rapinis, simul et Arriana impietate foedavit."

tained aspects of their own ethnic tradition which made them clearly identifiable to contemporaries, they also influenced each other in at least two fundamental aspects of their institutional life — religion and military affairs.

ALANS IN GAUL

When the Alans and Vandals crossed the Rhine in the winter of 406, the threat to Gaul was manifest to the Roman officials responsible for defense, and they worked diligently in the hope of gaining some of the invaders as allies. Goar, the Alan chief who came to terms with the empire, may not have been expected to have done so in light of the Alans' activities in Noricum and Raetia five years earlier, but once an agreement was reached little time seems to have been wasted in settling the newcomers for the defense of Gaul. The Rhine frontier was largely undefended; both the Franks, who dwelt along the river, and the second-line defenders, the Sarmatian military colonists (*laeti*), who had been settled further to the west during the fourth century, proved unable to stop the invaders in 406. These Sarmatians were established in colonies from Amiens in the north through Sermaise (Oise), Sermoise (Aisne), Rheims, Sermiers (Marne), Sermaize les Bains (Marne), and Langres in the south. These installations of *laeti* were positioned to protect important roads and cities, and there were also important workshops for the production of arms at Amiens, Soissons, and Rheims.[84]

With the aid of toponymical evidence it is possible to ascertain the probable location of at least some of the settlements established for Goar's followers. Allains (Somme) is located some thirty miles to the east of Amiens and protects the roads leading from Cologne to Amiens and Soissons. Twenty-five miles to the south-southeast is Alaincourt (Aisne) which commands the roads from Tournai to Soissons and Tournai to Rheims. Further to the southeast are Alland'huy (Ardennes) and another

---

84. Grenier, *Manuel d'archéologie*, V, 398ff; Stein, *Bas-empire*, I, 264; Bachrach, "Alans in Gaul," p. 478. Cf. H. Gröhler, *Ueber Ursprung und Bedeutung der französischen Ortsnamen*, II (Heidelberg, 1913–1935), 7, 295.

Alaincourt (Ardennes); both protect the road from Cologne to Rheims and are located thirty-five and twenty-five miles respectively from Rheims. To the south of Rheims are Allancourt (Marne) and Sampigny (Marne). Allancourt is only a few miles from Sermiers, mentioned above. Yet another Sampigny was established thirty miles east of Sermaize les Bains and commands the road from Toul to Verdun. The word *Sampigny* is derived from the Alan name Sambida, though the close linguistic relation of the Alan and Sarmatian languages makes it impossible to determine with certainty if the Sambidas for whom these towns were named were Alans or Sarmatians. On the high ground commanding the road from Metz through Verdun to Rheims is found Allamont (Meurthe-et-Moselle). To the south of Metz along the road to Toul lies Alaincourt-la-Côte (Meurthe-et-Moselle). Just to the south of Toul on the way to Langres are Alain (Meurthe-et-Moselle) and Aillianville (Haute-Marne); the latter commands the road to Verdun. The eastern approach to Langres is guarded by yet a third Alaincourt (Haute-Saône)[85] (see map 3).

While Goar and his followers were supporting the empire as allies, other Alans along with Vandals were ravaging parts of Gaul as was the usurper Constantine III. By 411 imperial power in Gaul had reached such a low point that Goar was encouraged to take overt action. In that year he joined with the Burgundian chief Gundahar to raise a Roman named Jovinus to the purple. Jovinus seems to have been proclaimed emperor at Monzen, a town some thirty miles east of the Burgundian headquarters at Waremme and some seventy-five miles east-northeast of Alaincourt (Aisne).[86]

As Jovinus's army moved south toward Arles, Athaulf, who

85. See appendix III, nos. 33, 9, 40, 10, 39, 55, 56, 37, 13, 8, 1, 12, respectively.
86. Olymp., *fr.* 17. Stein, *Bas-empire*, I, 264; H. Gregoire, "Où en est la question des Nibelungen?" *Byzantion*, X (1935), 219; and Bachrach, "Alans in Gaul," p. 478. Cf. Demougeot, *L'empire romain*, pp. 391, 502, and K. F. Stroheker, "Studien zu den historisch-geographischen Grundlagen der Nibelungendichtung," *Deutsche Vierteljahrschrift für Literaturwissenschaft und Geistesgeschichte*, XXXII (1958), 216–240. (This article has been reprinted in a collection of Stroheker's essays, *Germanentum und Spätantike* [Stuttgart, 1965], pp. 246–274.)

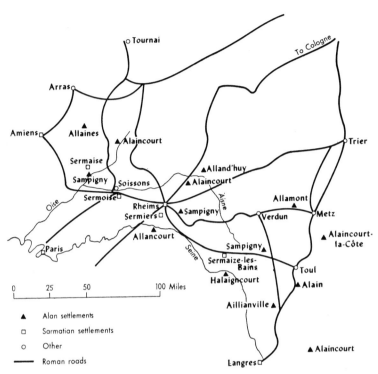

Map 3. Northeastern Gaul

succeeded Alaric as king of the Visigoths, came to join him. It should be recalled that a strong group of Alan cavalry had been united with these Goths at least from the days of the battle of Adrianople in 378. In any event, a disagreement developed between Jovinus and Athaulf, who then made an agreement with Rome to help the empire to eliminate Jovinus. When this was accomplished, Goar's Alans, like the rest of Jovinus's supporters, returned to their settlements in northern Gaul leaving the south to Athaulf and his followers. It seems unlikely that Goar regarded Jovinus as an usurper. Jovinus was a Roman, and to the untutored Alan chief a Roman close at hand must have been more real than someone far off in Ravenna. When Jovinus failed, Goar

61

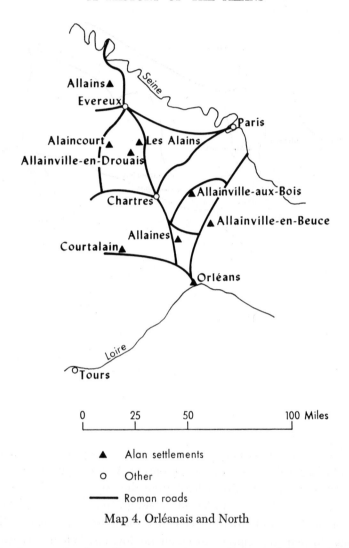

Map 4. Orléanais and North

simply remained in Roman service; in his mind he probably never left it.[87]

For a quarter of a century Goar and his Alans remained loyal supporters of the empire, although their neighbors the Burgundians revolted and were crushed by Aetius and his Hunnic allies.

87. Stein, *Bas-empire*, I, 264, and Bachrach, "Alans in Gaul," pp. 278–279. Gregory, *Hist.*, II, 9.

The Alans Come to the West

In approximately 442, after it became clear to Aetius that he could no longer rely upon the Huns for support, he turned to Goar and convinced him to move some of his people to settlements in the Orléanais in order to control the *bacaudae* of Armorica and to keep the Visigoths from expanding their territories northward across the Loire.[88]

Goar settled a substantial number of his followers in the Orléanais and the area to the north and personally moved his own capital to the city of Orléans. The toponymical evidence helps us to identify some of the places in which the Alans probably settled: Alains (Eure), Alaincourt (Eure), Les Allains (Eure), Allainville-en-Drouais (Eure-et-Loir), Allainville aux Bois (Seine-et-Oise), Allainville-en-Beuce (Loiret), Courtalain (Eure-et-Loir), and Allaines (Eure-et-Loir) (see map 4).[89]

Aetius issued orders for the magnates in the area mentioned above to divide their lands with the Alans and accept them as guests. A significant number of the magnates, however, refused to obey this decree and resisted the Alans by force. Goar then found it necessary to drive out the resisters. By doing this he seems to have earned himself a bad reputation among some of the Gallo-Roman aristocracy. The author of the *Querolus*, a Latin comedy written shortly after these events, alludes to the disruption which may have been caused in part by the Alans; and Salvian, a priest from Marseilles, condemns them for their rapacity.[90]

By driving out a significant number of the Gallo-Roman magnates, the Alans acquired most of the lands instead of only a

88. Bachrach, "Alans in Gaul," p. 481. *Chron. Gall.*, ch. 127: "Alani, quibus terrae Galliae ulterioris cum incolis dividendae a patricio Aetio traditae fuerant, resistentes armis subigunt et expulsis dominis terrae possessionem vi adipiscuntur."
89. See appendix III, nos. 14, 11, 34, 36, 15, 35, 46, 32, respectively.
90. *Chron. Gall.*, ch. 127. Bachrach, "Alans in Gaul," p. 483; F. L. Ganshof, "Note sur le sens de 'Ligeris' au titre XLVII de la loi salique et dans le 'Querolus,'" *Historical Essays in Honour of James Tait* (Manchester, 1933), pp. 112–117; *Aulularia sive Querolus*, pp. 16–17; L. Havet, *Le Querolus* (Paris, 1880), pp. 216–218; Salvian, *De gub. Dei*, IV, 14; and Nora K. Chadwick, *Early Brittany* (Cardiff, 1969), pp. 150ff. For an early fifth-century date for the *Querolus* see F. Corsaro, *Querolus. Studio introduttivo e commentario* (Bologna, 1965), pp. 7–12.

share of them as well as the economic dependents who worked these lands. The relatively large number of Alan place names surviving in this area may perhaps be explained by the fact that many of the Gallo-Roman magnates were driven out; thus, among the important people who would be likely to give their names to villas, there were more Alans than there would have been had the original owners remained.

The Alan settlements from Orléans in the south to Alains on the Seine in the north were arranged in part to help control the *bacaudae* of Armorica. By situating the Alans thusly the *Tractus Armoricani* was divided into two parts; the Alans were then in a good position to keep the *bacaudae* in the western part of the *Tractus* from uniting with those in the eastern part. The Alans could attack either group without having to face a unified enemy in force. The southern terminus of this line of Alan settlements was the well-fortified and strategically placed city of Orléans. To the north of Orléans was Allaines whose strategic importance was recognized throughout the Middle Ages. Its medieval fortifications are still standing. Unfortunately, there has not been enough archaeological investigation to ascertain what, if any, implacements at Allaines or for that matter at any of the other places with Alan names can be traced back to the fifth century.[91]

In 445–446, the Armoricans rebelled against Roman rule, and Aetius ordered Goar to punish them. As a reward for the service which Aetius asked of them, the Alans were promised the wealth which would be confiscated from the rebels. Goar called together the Alans from their settlements in the Orléanais. Surrounded by his personal followers who were quartered with him at Orléans, he took to the road to crush the Armorican rebels. While on the march Goar's column, mounted and in full armor, was halted by Bishop Germanus who tried to dissuade the Alan chief from attacking the rebels. After a conversation carried on through an interpreter, Goar seems to have consented to withhold his attack if Aetius, the commander in Gaul who had given the orders for the campaign, agreed to withdraw the orders. Germanus then set out for Ravenna to talk with Galla Placidia in order to obtain

91. Bachrach, "Alans in Gaul," p. 481. See appendix III, no. 32.

a pardon for the Armoricans. He never obtained the pardon, however, and sometime before 450 Goar subdued the rebels.[92]

Shortly before 451, however, Goar ceased to rule over the Alans of the Orléanais, and he was replaced by Sangiban. The sources do not mention Goar's death, although he was a well-known figure in Gaul for more than four decades and of advanced age. He had been a chief since at least 406. By heading the campaign of 446, Goar had shown that he was still capable of leading his men into battle. It will be remembered that the Alans did not venerate their aged warriors who lived on past their ability to fight, but chose their leaders from those most able in military matters. By 451 Goar may well have still been living but, because he was no longer able to take the field at the head of his troops, he was probably replaced by a new chief. Since the aged Goar was no longer prominent, perhaps even scorned by his own people, his demise would not have readily found its way into the writings of contemporary observers.[93]

In 451, Sangiban was called upon by the empire to help to defend Gaul against the invasions of Attila's Huns. The Huns laid siege to Orléans, Sangiban's headquarters, and after many days of bitter fighting the city was on the verge of being taken. The Gothic historian, Jordanes, who wrote during the mid-sixth century, contends that Sangiban's loyalty to Rome was suspect and that he conspired to surrender Orléans to the Huns without a fight. Jordanes goes on to say that it was only the timely arrival of the Romans and Visigoths under Aetius's command that saved the city. Other accounts of this event indicate that Orléans underwent a bloody siege and was bravely defended against the onslaughts of the Huns and their allies. Sidonius Apollinaris, a Gallo-Roman living at the time of the battle and one who had no love for either the Visigoths or the Alans, maintains that the Visigoths' hesitation in taking the field was responsible for At-

92. V. Germani, ch. 28. E. A. Thompson, "A Chronological Note on St. Germanus of Auxerre," Analecta Bollandiana, LXXV (1957), 136–137; and Bachrach, "Alans in Gaul," pp. 481–482. Merobaudes, Panegyric, 2.8, may refer to this. See F. Clover, Flavius Merobaudes, in Transactions of the American Philosophical Society, LXI (1971), 48–49.

93. Bachrach, "Alans in Gaul," p. 484.

tila's near success at Orléans. It would seem that Jordanes's pro-Gothic sentiments encouraged him to make the Visigoths heroes at the expense of the Alans to whom they were hostile. Aside from Jordanes's apparently prejudiced account, it is generally agreed that the city underwent a bloody siege, and there is no reason to believe that Sangiban was treacherous in this instance. The possibility should not be discounted, however, that as the siege wore on and defeat seemed certain because of the Visigoths' lack of interest in helping against the Huns, the Alan chief may have contemplated or even discussed surrender with his advisers.[94]

But the Romans and Visigoths did reach Orléans in time, and after turning back the Huns, Aetius and his allies, now including a noteworthy contingent of Alans, pursued Attila's forces to Châlons. In the famous battle of Châlons Western Europe was saved from the Hunnic menace, and the Alans played an important role in the encounter. Sangiban's forces held the middle of the allied line with the Romans on their right and the Goths on their left. At the center of the Hunnic line was Attila with his most formidable followers. The Romans on the right wing held the high ground and repulsed the enemy attack, while the Alans at the center held firm against Attila's onslaught. Once the enemy attack had been blunted and stalled, the Goths, according to Jordanes, charged from their left-wing position and in a flanking movement routed the Huns. The steadfast and effective performance of Sangiban's Alans in the face of the most dangerous element in Attila's forces suggests that Jordanes's assertion to the effect that Aetius placed the Alans in the middle of the line so that they would not be able to flee is simply another of the Gothic writer's prejudiced sallies against the Alans.[95]

Sometime in the next two years, according to Jordanes, the

94. Jordanes, *Getica*, XXXVII; Sidonius Apollinaris, *Carm.*, VII, ll. 328ff, and *Epist.*, VIII, 15, 1; Gregory, *Hist.*, II, 7. Bachrach, "Alans in Gaul," p. 483. Cf. A. Loyen, "Le rôle de Saint Aignan dans la défense d'Orléans," *Comptes Rendus: Académie des inscriptions et Belles-Lettres* (Paris, 1969), pp. 64–74.
95. Jordanes, *Getica*, XXXVIII, XXXIX, XL. Täckholm, "Catalaunian Fields," pp. 259–276, ignores the role played by the Alans.

Alans, the Huns, and the Visigoths were once again involved in military operations against each other. He writes that in this episode, Attila, after his limited successes in Italy, threatened the Emperor Marcian because he had refused to pay the tribute promised by his predecessor Theodosius II. While the Romans were preparing to deal with a Hunnic thrust into the East, Attila once again moved west into Gaul in the hopes of defeating those Alans settled in northern Aquitaine. According to Jordanes, if this attack succeeded, the entire defensive system in this part of Gaul would be endangered, and the Visigoths would be severely threatened. Jordanes's implication that the Alans were the key to the "Roman" defense of Aquitaine should not be overlooked. In any event, Jordanes tells us that the Visigothic King Thorismud learned of Attila's plans and led his troops northward to the Alan settlements on the left bank of the Loire. Jordanes contends that a battle took place (one very similar to that which had been fought at Châlons) in which Thorismud destroyed Attila's hopes of victory, routed him, and forced him to evacuate the area. After this Jordanes eulogizes the Visigoths: "Thus while the famous Attila, lord of many victories, tried to erase the fame of his conquerors [the Visigoths] and tried to wipe out thusly the defeat he had suffered [at Châlons] at the hands of the Visigoths; he was defeated again and retreated without glory." Jordanes follows this paean with a very curious sentence: "Thorismud, having driven out the Hunnic band by using Alans, left for Toulouse without having lost any of his own men."[96]

This account by Jordanes, although intended to glorify Thorismud and the Visigoths, does no such thing when read carefully. Beneath Jordanes's panegyric is a very clear indication that the Alans were the immediate object of the Hunnic attack and that the Alans drove off the Huns without Visigothic help — none of Thorismud's men were lost in battle. Jordanes seems to have inflated to heroic and epic proportions a factual account of an Alan-Hunnic encounter by embroidering it with praise for the Visigoths and King Thorismud. It is very unlikely, however, that

96. Jordanes, *Getica*, XXXVIII, XXXIX, XL.

Attila himself actually invaded the north of Aquitaine in 452–453, but it is possible that a band of his followers had remained in Gaul after the battle of Châlons in 451 and were defeated by the Alans during the following year.[97]

In either 452 or the next year, Thorismud did move north and attack the Alans. In this campaign he defeated them, according to Gregory of Tours, and drove them from northern Aquitaine. The absence of Alan place names on the left bank of the Loire suggests that Thorismud was very effective in driving out the Alans whom he had defeated. It is certain, however, that the Alan capital at Orléans was not taken by Goths who, after securing the Loire as a northern border, turned their attention to Spain and left the Alans across the river in peace.[98]

In a small area encompassing part of northwestern Switzerland near Lake Geneva and the département Ain further to the west in France, there are some place names which might indicate an erstwhile Alan settlement. About twenty-five miles northeast of Lyons is a cluster of three small towns: Alain, Aleins, and Alaniers. Some twenty-five miles to the east-northeast on the outskirts of Bourg is the town of Allaigne. Across the border in Switzerland, some thirty miles further east and within the environs of Geneva, is a river formerly called Aqua de Alandons, while further to the north and east only five or so miles north of Lausanne is the town of Allens.[99]

Archaeological evidence lends some support to the possibility that these place names indicate an early medieval settlement of Alans. Scattered throughout this area are a significant number of deformed skull burials. The practice of deforming the skull of young children by binding them tightly with cloth or rawhide has long been identified as a custom practiced by some central Asiatic nomads. Some groups which had become part of the Alan people are known to have practiced this custom. The burials

97. Hodgkin, *Italy and Her Invaders*, II, 170; Levison, "Germanus von Auxerre," p. 136, n. 7; Robert Reynolds and Robert Lopez, "Odoacer: German or Hun?" *AHR*, LII (1946), 36–53.
98. Gregory, *Hist.*, II, 7; Jordanes, *Getica*, XLIV. Bachrach, "Alans in Gaul," p. 482.
99. See appendix III, nos. 6, 24, 20, 28, 42, 49, respectively.

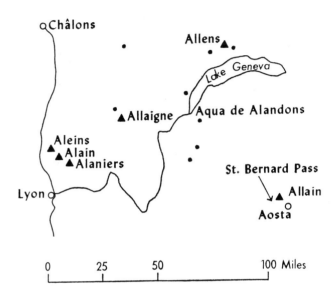

Map 5. Swiss Border

in the area under discussion date from the middle part of the
fifth century and are thoroughly interspersed in the vicinity of
the places which have Alan names (see map 5, and map 6 for
additional archaeological evidence from the later seventh century.)[100]

In 443 the Roman government resettled a group of Burgundians in this general area. Previously these same Burgundians had
lived along the middle Rhine in close proximity to Goar's Alans.
These Alans and Burgundians were both allies of Rome and

100. Eric Dingwall, *Artificial Cranial Deformation* (London, 1931), and
Werner, *Attila-Reiches*, pp. 5–18.

69

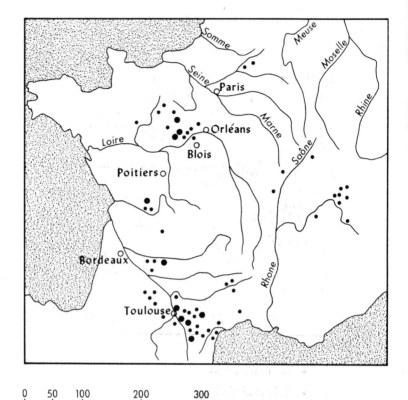

0   50   100   200   300
|____|____|_____|_____|
              Miles

• 1 or 2 objects

● 3 or more objects

Map 6. Alan Archaeological Evidence in Gaul

worked together for more than a generation. It seems reasonable in light of the place names and archaeological evidence that a small group of Alans attached themselves to the main group of Burgundians who moved into the Savoy area in 443.

When these settlements are plotted on a map or, to be more exact, when these place names and deformed head burials are plotted on a map, they show that the suggested Alan military colonies protected the northern approaches to the Saint Bernard

Pass. This road to Italy is protected on the southern side by the Alan settlements of Allain, five miles north of Aosta, and Alagna, thirty miles to the east[101] (see map 5). Such a strategic placement of settlements seems consistent with Aetius's plans in the early 440s when he moved two groups of Alans, one into Orléanais and the other into the Valentinois, so that they would be strategically located for the defense of the empire.

CONCLUSIONS

The Alans' trek westward and their settlement within the empire illustrate both continuity with the customs of the steppes and digressions from them in assimilating new ways of living. While on the steppes, the Alans never were unified politically into a horde as were the Huns or Avars. The exigencies of nomadic life require that the wandering bands be of rather limited size, and the conditions which make possible the formation of a nomadic horde apparently never developed among the Alans. Thus, in coming west they generally joined with other peoples, like the Visigoths or Vandals; or in small groups they entered imperial military service. The mélange nature of the Alan groups, being bound together as they were by common customs rather than by physiognomical similarities, presumably did not obstruct such unions with non-Alans and may even have facilitated these alliances.

In the early period of settlement all the Alan groups at one time or another showed their desire to become a part of the empire, to defend it, and to enjoy its benefits. Some groups, because of events beyond their control, never did fulfill this desire, while others were very successful in doing so. Those who settled in Italy and Gaul were able to serve the empire and benefit from this service though they did not accept Christianity immediately or even learn Latin. Other Alans, like those who went to Spain and then to Africa, never were able to find lasting peace with the empire though they did in fact become Christian,

101. See above, n. 41.

that is, Arian Christians. At Constantinople the Alans were very powerful and for a time their leaders in effect ruled though did not reign over the eastern empire. There too the Alans or at least some of them became Arian Christians, intermarrying with elite elements in both the Roman and German segments of the population.

The failure of the Alans in Spain, Africa, and Constantinople may be contrasted with the success of those in Italy and Gaul, if success is to be characterized in terms of survival and integration. Survival seems to be a general human value and assimilation and integration seem to have been particularly Alan values. Those Alans who were unsuccessful seem in general to have been a powerful threat to the empire, while those who were successful remained little or no threat to the empire. The ultimate destruction of the unsuccessful Alan groups was brought about by the actions of the eastern part of the empire, the half which flourished. The Alans in Italy and Gaul lived in the weaker western part of the empire which finally was divided among the various invaders who conquered it.

These general remarks should not obscure some fundamental developments among the Alans in the West and especially those who succeeded. Within two generations of their coming west the Alans changed from nomadic warrior-herders to sedentary landholders sharing the wealth with the Roman *potentiores*. On the steppes the Alans of fighting age had been a warrior elite and when they settled down they retained much of this form of social organization. To continue the effective use of their vaunted cavalry tactics, the Alan horsemen needed the opportunity to train and the means to keep their horses, arms, and armor. The leisure to devote one's time and effort to training in the art of war and the wealth to possess horses, arms, and armor were beyond the means of a fifth-century peasant burdened by agricultural duties or immobilized by the limitations of serfdom. The freedom from economic need which enabled the Alans to maintain themselves as fighting men was provided by the imperial hospitality system which brought them into the Roman social structure at the higher levels of society. Therefore, the Alans as an erstwhile, nomadic warrior elite became a settled, landholding warrior class. Among the crumbling ruin of Roman institutions the Alans, especially those in Gaul, were in a good position to become a part of a new medieval aristocracy.

CHAPTER III

The Assimilation
of the Alans

I N GAUL by the end of the fifth century, contemporaries ceased to refer to the Alans as an identifiable tribal entity. This may be interpreted in any of three ways: the Alans migrated from Gaul, they were annihilated, or they were assimilated by the surrounding populations. Since there is no evidence that they were annihilated or that they emigrated, it seems reasonable to investigate the possibility that they were assimilated. The survival of several dozen place names which can be attributed either to Alan influence or to their direct settlement strongly suggests that the Alans did not simply pack up and leave after living in Gaul for three generations. This toponymical evidence, which was discussed in the previous chapter, may be contrasted with the legacy of place names of the Visigothic settlements in Aquitaine. Although the Goths were far more numerous than were the Alans and their settlement in Aquitaine endured for a century, their impact upon the toponymy was considerably less impressive than that of the Alans. The survival and wide use of Alan personal names also imply continued Alan influence. For example, Alain and its variants Allain, Alan, and Allan, all of which are derived from the Latin *Alanus,* remain popular as both Christian and family names. In Aquitaine and in the area north of the Loire the name Goar seems to be used quite frequently as well.[1]

1. Wallace-Hadrill, *Long-Haired Kings,* p. 30; Bachrach, "Armorican Chivalry," p. 169; Bachrach, "Alans in Gaul," p. 481.

The first step on the road to assimilation was taken by the Alans within a generation of their coming west when they settled down as guests under the imperial hospitality system. Therefore, they gave up their nomadic ways and accommodated themselves to the sedentary landholding way of life which prevailed in the later Roman empire and its successor states in the West.

The second major phase in the process of assimilation was the Alans' acceptance of Christianity, and in particular orthodox Christianity. Toward the middle of the fifth century the Alans in Gaul were still pagans, but by the end of the century they had become Christians. By the second half of the sixth century those who spoke of religion classified the Alans as Christians. Martin of Braga could, in good conscience, attribute the conversion of the Alans to the efforts of St. Martin of Tours who died in 397. Martin of Braga would not have been able to do this if the true date of their conversion were known or if it were a part of the living popular memory. He certainly could not have spoken about the Alans as Christians had they been known to be pagans. If the true conversion date were known or if they were still pagans, then St. Martin could not possibly have been responsible for their conversion — a conversion, incidentally, of which he was wholly innocent. Fortunatus, a contemporary of Martin of Braga, was particularly well informed about affairs in what is today western France; he lists the Alans among those barbarians who had become Christians. The attribution of the Alans' conversion to St. Martin and the failure of either Fortunatus or Martin of Braga to condemn them for being Arians (as Bede condemns the Alans who went to Africa) indicate that the Alans who had settled in Gaul became orthodox Christians.[2]

The example of St. Goar illustrates this process of assimilation. Goar was born in Aquitaine in the first half of the sixth century during the reign of Clovis's son Childebert. Goar's parents had both been given Roman names, but they remembered their Alan

2. Fortunatus, *In laudem Sanctae Mariae*, ll. 287–291; Martin of Braga, p. 282. E. Dekkers, *Clavis Patrum Latinorum* (2nd ed.), in *Sacris erudiri*, III (Steenbrugge, 1961), no. 1044a; Bachrach, "Alans in Gaul," pp. 486–487. For Arian Alans, see Bede, *Chron.*, ch. 480.

heritage by naming their son Goar, perhaps to honor the memory of the famous chief of their grandparents' era. The young Goar, whose parents or more probably grandparents had accepted the orthodox Christianity of Rome and rejected the Arianism of the Visigoths, became a priest and a missionary.[3]

In any discussion of assimilation, distinguishing physical characteristics such as hair color, complexion, or height must be taken into consideration. Ammianus Marcellinus claimed that the Alans were tall and tended to have blond hair. This, if true, would make them not unlike many of the Germanic peoples who settled in Gaul. Claudian, however, in describing an Alan leader known for his military prowess notes that he was short in stature. In fact, this particular Alan seems to fit the general descriptions given by contemporaries of Huns. Two pictorial representations of Alans survive. One, a disc honoring the consulship of Aspar in 434, depicts him along with his father, Ardaburius, and a German named Plinthas. Nothing about the appearance of the Alans on this disc differentiates them physically from either German chiefs or Roman generals. A second representation purports to picture Alan and Vandal prisoners captured in 416. There is, however, no way to distinguish on phenotypical grounds between those who are Vandals and those who are Alans. This type of pictorial evidence must be used very carefully since artistic conventions during this period tended to present people in a rather stylized manner (see plates 1 and 2).[4]

Perhaps the most important indication that the Alans lacked any phenotypical characteristics which differentiated them greatly from their contemporaries is the silence of these very contemporaries on such matters. That the Alans were not a clearly

3. *V. Goar.*, ch. 1: "In diebus Childeberti regis Francorum, filio Chlodoveo, erat vir venerabilis nomine Goar, homo Aquitanicus, cuius pater vocatur Georgius et mater eius Valeria." See Bachrach, "Alans in Gaul," p. 486. There is some argument concerning Goar's dates; for further discussion of this problem see Krusch's introduction to the *Vita*, pp. 404–405.

4. Ammianus Marcellinus, XXXI, 2, 21; Claudian, *De Bel. Goth.*, ll. 580ff. For the pictorial representations see Delbrueck, *Die Consular Diptychen*, pp. 154–155, pl. 35, p. 92. See also Courtois, *Les Vandales*, p. 54; Gautier, *Genséric*, pp. 239–240; Richard Frank, *Scholae Palatinae* (Rome, 1969), p. 202.

distinguishable phenotypic group may in addition be inferred from the very essence of their pattern of social organization: the Alans as a people were drawn from many groups; their identity was essentially based upon cultural patterns rather than upon so-called "racial characteristics."

THE ALANS OF ARMORICA

During the second half of the fifth century, the Alans in Gaul were assimilated into the populations of the areas in which they had settled. Those in the Orléanais were becoming identified with the *Armorici*, the inhabitants of the *Tractus Armoricani*. The *Armorici* were also a composite of many peoples, including erstwhile imperial troops who originally had been drawn from throughout the empire, fugitives from Britain, and Gallo-Romans; these groups, as well as the Alans, some Franks, and perhaps others, had been subject to varying degrees of Romanization. This mélange of peoples known as the *Armorici* owed their loyalty to the empire in the hectic decades following the battle of Châlons in 451 and supported Aegidius, the Roman military commander in Gaul who had his headquarters at Soissons.[5]

While the Alans of the Orléanais were being Armoricanized, their headquarters at Orléans was the target of Visigothic expansionism. Aegidius, however, helped to protect Orléans on at least one occasion when the Visigothic Prince Frederic, the brother of King Theuderic, was killed. The Franks of Tournai, after breaking with Aegidius's son and successor, Syagrius, also became involved in attacks into Armorica. Childeric attacked Orléans about 466 and a year or two later he allied with the Saxons settled on the islands in the mouth of the Loire River to attack the Alans. These attempts to seize control of the Orléanais where the descendants of Goar's Alans held sway were unsuccessful.[6]

5. Bachrach, "Alans in Gaul," pp. 487–488, and "Procopius and the Chronology of Clovis's Reign," *Viator*, I (1970), 21–31.
6. Gregory, *Hist.*, II, 19, as in II, 9, confuses Alaman and Alan. The former text which was probably drawn from local annals, perhaps from Angers, has been the subject of much discussion but is still in need of further study. On these texts, see W. Junghans, "Histoire Critique des

Clovis, Childeric's son and successor, led a number of raids into Armorica, and in approximately 502–503 he organized a concerted effort to bring the area under his control. Though Clovis's forces were defeated by the Armoricans, a treaty was arranged by which the Armoricans recognized Clovis's leadership. A later contemporary, Procopius, observes that the orthodox Christianity of both the Armoricans and of Clovis's followers made them natural allies against the Arian Visigoths to the south. In addition, the Alans of the Orléanais, now a part of the *Armorici,* had always been loyal to the empire; their alliance and Clovis's planned campaign against the Visigoths were strongly supported by the Emperor Anastasius at Constantinople.[7]

The impact of the alliance with the Armoricans upon Clovis's future was at least as great as his impact upon them. In 496 when Clovis accepted Christianity and tried to get his supporters to follow him into the baptismal font, only about half of them went. The other three thousand or so Frankish warriors led by the *regulus* Ragnachar defected. As a result, Clovis's military strength was severely weakened and his campaigns against the Burgundians in 500–501 and against the Armoricans in 503–504 ended in military failure. Without the several thousand Alan horsemen upon whom Clovis could rely after the treaty with the Armoricans, he could scarcely have posed a real threat to the Visigoths. The importance of Clovis's newly acquired cavalry is illustrated by a surviving order issued by him for the campaign of 507 against the Visigoths. Clovis decreed that his horsemen might take only grass and water for their mounts when they were crossing church lands. Clovis seems to have been responding to the pleas of bishops who were conversant with the Alan

règnes de Childeric et de Chlodovech," trans. and augmented by G. Monod, *BEHE*, XXXVII (1879), 12–15, and L. Lair, "Conjectures sur les chapitres XVIII et XIX du livre II de l'*Historia Ecclesiastica* de Grégoire de Tours," *Annuaire-Bulletin de la Société de l'Histoire de France*, XXXV (1898), 3–29.

7. Procopius, *B.G.*, I, xii, 8ff. This is discussed in detail by Bachrach, "Clovis's Reign," pp. 21–31. On Anastasius's support, see Gregory, *Hist.*, II, 38, and the discussion by Wallace-Hadrill, *Long-Haired Kings*, pp. 174–176.

reputation for rapaciousness that was well known throughout Gaul during the mid-fifth century.[8]

Before the end of the fifth century some of the Alans of the Orléanais began moving westward into Breton-dominated parts of Armorica. A medieval Armorican chronicle preserves the tradition that the Breton chief Audren (d. ca. 464) ruled over some Alans. In the Le Mans area, between the settlements of the Orléanais and Audren's territory, Alan influence is observable in the early sixth century. It was then that a bishop named *Alanus* first served at the city of Le Mans.[9]

A little to the east of Audren's lands was the town of Alangavia (modern Langeais). Langeais is about eight miles west of Tours along the Loire. During the latter part of the sixth century, Gregory of Tours mentions Alangavia twice, but neither time does he suggest that it was a recent establishment; it may well have been founded during the latter part of the fifth century when some groups of Alans were moving west from Orléans. It seems possible that the Alans who settled Alangavia were trying to sustain their identity in a situation in which they were rapidly being assimilated.[10]

Such antiquarianism in the naming of a new settlement by a people well along the road to assimilation should not be surprising. It was possibly just this kind of desire to preserve some contact with a past identity during the crucial period before that past was totally lost which motivated St. Goar's parents to give him an Alan name even though the family had been using Roman names for at least a generation and had been Christian probably for two generations.

8. Bachrach, "Clovis's Reign," pp. 29–30; "Alans in Gaul," p. 487; and Gregory, *Hist.*, II, 37: "ut nullus de regione illa aliud quam herbarum alimenta aquamque praesumeret." For further discussion of Clovis's forces, see Bernard S. Bachrach, "Procopius, Agathias, and the Frankish Military," *Speculum*, XLV (1970), 435–441, and *Merovingian Military Organization* (Minneapolis, 1972), ch. I.

9. P. H. Morice, *Histoire ecclésiastique et civile de Bretagne*, I (Guincamp, 1835), 11, provides information from the chronicle mentioned above. He does not indicate its name, location, or date, nor does he mention if it had been published. A. de Martonne, "Deux nouveaux évêques du Mans," *Revue historique de l'ouest*, I (1885), 506–515.

10. See appendix III, no. 52.

Additional evidence for Alan movement westward is provided by place names. To the west of Alangavia along the coast between Nantes and Vannes is the town of Alain (Loire-Inférieure). About twenty-five miles north-northwest of Vannes lies Allain (Morbihan), and twenty miles further north was the medieval town of Alanczon (Morbihan) which today is called Bodieuc. Thirty-five miles west of Alanczon is Goarec (Côtes-du-Nord). Further to the north and east in Calvados is Allain.[11]

Toward the middle of the sixth century a magnate named Conomor ruled much of western Armorica including the area from Carhaix to Dol in the north and as far east and south as Vannes. The lives of the Breton saints which provide the bulk of the evidence for Conomor's career characterize him as a foreigner, probably from Cornwall. Modern scholars have identified him as Mark Conomor who ruled also at Carhays in Cornwall. Conomor is described by late contemporaries as an usurper and is charged with the murder of a certain Jonas who ruled the area around Dol. After taking over Jonas's lands, Conomor is said to have exiled his son to the Frankish realm of King Childebert I. Childebert had the youth imprisoned. The exiled prince was named Alan Judual, the first of some half dozen counts and dukes in Brittany during the early Middle Ages to bear the name Alanus.[12]

The lands ruled by Conomor were inhabited by a heterogeneous population including Celts, Romans, Germans, and Alans. A reliable tradition recorded in the life of St. Paul of Léon indicates that four different languages were spoken in Conomor's Armorican lands, indicating that in the mid-sixth century there were still those of Alan descent who spoke their mother tongue.[13]

11. *Ibid.*, nos. 7, 30, 44, 48, 29, respectively.
12. *V. Samson*, chs. 55–59; Gregory, *Hist.*, IV, 3. Morice, *Bretagne*, I, 50; Nora K. Chadwick, "The Colonization of Brittany from Celtic Britain," *Proceedings of the British Academy*, LX (1965), 279–280; and *Early Brittany*, pp. 212ff. See also *V. Paul.*, ch. 8.
13. *V. Paul.*, ch. 22: "Interea cum haec et alia multa bona opera, Dei gratia cooperante, in illo agebantur, fama ejus regis Maric pervolant ad aures, quem alio nomine *Quonomonum* vocant. Qui eo tempore, amplissimi producto sub limite regendo moenia sceptri, vir magnus imperiali potentia atque potentissimus habebatur, ita ut quatuor linguae diversarum gentium

THE ASSIMILATION OF THE ALANS

In Armorica at this time one finds among the many medieval stories that were intended to explain the origins of the peoples of Europe several tales which give special prominence to the Alans. The one under consideration here survives because it was included by Nennius in his *Historia Brittonum* for the purpose of illustrating the origins of the English people. The original, which Nennius incorporated into his work, dated from the first half of the sixth century and was considered by Ferdinand Lot to have been the work of a priest of Alan descent living in Armorica. This story, primarily in the form of a genealogy, is aimed in part at demonstrating the relation of all peoples to God. It accords to the Alans a position of primacy vis-à-vis the other peoples of Europe. The story expands upon the biblical tradition that Noah's son Japhet repopulated Europe after the flood and it credits Japhet with having an heir named Alanus who was the first man to dwell in Europe. He had three sons, Hisicon, Armenon, and Neugio; these in turn had among their descendants the Vandals, Franks, Latins, Alamans, Britons, Burgundians, and Goths.[14]

Although the Alan priest who composed this list knew that the *Alani* had no nation of their own, he nevertheless seems to have felt that they should be given an important place in history. Thus he makes the eponymous founder of the *Alani* the ancestor of

uno ejus subjacerent imperio." The editor Dom Plaine (p. 222, n. 1) suggests that the four languages were those of the Picts, Britons, Scots, and Angles. Modern scholarship, however, has shown extensive Latin linguistic survival in the land ruled by Conomor. The Angles never penetrated into Conomor's territory although the Franks and other Germanic-speaking groups did. In addition, scholars have now shown that all the Celtic dialects in Conomor's lands were mutually intelligible and did not at that time constitute "linguae diversae." Thus, three of the four languages mentioned in the *Vita* have been accounted for: Latin, Frankish, and Celtic. The fourth would reasonably seem to have been Alanic. On these linguistic problems, see Chadwick, "Colonization," pp. 270–273; J. L. Fleuriot, "Recherches sur les enclaves romanes anciennes en territoire brettonant," *Études celtiques.* VIII (1958), 164ff; and Kenneth Jackson, *Language and History in Early Britain* (Cambridge, Mass., 1953), pp. 27–30.

14. Nennius, ch. 17. F. Lot, *Nennius et l'Historia Brittonum,* I (Paris, 1934), 50. Cf. Robert Hanning, *The Vision of History in Early Britain* (New York, 1966), p. 106. Cf. H. M. Chadwick, *Early Scotland* (Cambridge, 1949), pp. 81–88.

all the nations of Europe. It cannot be ascertained whether this priest was in fact aware that the Alans did play a role among the Vandals, Goths, Romans, Burgundians, and Franks; it is more than likely that he was simply indulging in ethnocentric historiography. It should be noted, however, that the currency of a story in Armorica which gives the *Alani* primacy in Europe points up the existence of strong pro-Alan influences there at about the same time that a ruling house of sorts with at least nominal Alan connections was struggling for survival against an usurper from Cornwall. The later acceptance of this story by a British historian of the early ninth century with a lively interest in Armorica suggests that Alan influences in Brittany continued to survive.

The theory that was propagated in Armorica during the mid-sixth century of the Alan origin of the peoples of Europe was not accepted further to the east. During the next century the chronicler Fredegar wrote of the Trojan origin of the Franks. His is apparently the first attempt to identify the Franks with the glories of classical antiquity. As found in Fredegar's work, Priam was the first king of the Franks. His people divided into several groups, one of which was the *Frigii*, who, under their leader Francio, ravaged a portion of Asia and then moved into Europe where they settled in the area between the Rhine, the Danube, and the sea. Fredegar continues by telling of Francio's death and the division of the Frankish people into groups led by dukes. These groups are depicted as fighting very successfully against the Romans. Further in the story we learn that the Franks and the Romans are cousins since Friga and Aeneas were both sons of Priam.[15]

It must be noted, however, that Fredegar did not permit the Trojan origin of the Franks to cut them off from the biblical tradition. He includes in his chronicle a version of the *Liber Generationis* in which there is a list of peoples who are said to be descended from Japhet, the son of Noah responsible for re-

15. See the discussion by Wallace-Hadrill, *Long-Haired Kings,* pp. 79–83.

THE ASSIMILATION OF THE ALANS

populating Europe. Fredegar interpolated into this list the *Troiane* and the *Frigiiae* and thus affirmed both the Trojan origins of the Franks and their biblical respectability. Fredegar did not utilize the Armorican tradition developed during the previous century which grants the Alans primacy in the repopulation of Europe.[16] Another Armorican tradition is of interest in this context. This one, also preserved by Nennius in his *Historia Brittonum,* gives the Alans a position of primacy in Europe at the expense of historically more important peoples. In the texts used by Nennius, an effort was made to demonstrate the Trojan origin of the Britons. Thus the Britons, through their eponymous founder Brutus, are descended from Hisicon through *Alanus,* eventually to Aeneas and Troius, and ultimately to Japhet. This story combines the biblical, Roman, and Trojan themes of British origins, and, as in the purely biblical effort discussed above, *Alanus* remains anterior to the existing nations of Europe. It is therefore evident that the kind of heritage for which both the Franks and the Britons were striving was in the Armorican tradition assured to the Alans earlier than to any of the other peoples of Europe.[17]

In one case, the Armorican tradition which emphasizes *Alanus* places the peoples of Europe including the Franks in a subordinate position, while in another instance it ignores the Franks completely. Fredegar dwells upon Frankish importance in his genealogical tales and ignores the Alans. The obvious bias of regional preference—the Alans were influential in Armorica and the Franks dominant further to the east — does not seem adequate to explain these two traditions when more of the evidence is scrutinized. Fredegar was a strong supporter of the idea of Frankish greatness. As the originator or, at the least, as the popularizer of the story of the Franks' Trojan origins, he connected them to the glory of classical antiquity; in showing that they defeated the Romans he praised their military prowess; and in a rhetorical flourish he lauds them as militarily superior to all. Perhaps only in the expanded prologue of *Lex Salica,* which was

16. *Ibid.*
17. Nennius, chs. 7, 17, 18.

composed in an even more ethnocentrically Frankish milieu than that in which the genealogy of Fredegar was composed, are the Franks more highly praised.[18] It should be of little surprise to learn, therefore, that the bloody defeat inflicted upon the Franks by the Alans in 406, an event recorded by Gregory of Tours whom Fredegar epitomizes, is conveniently omitted by the latter.

Frankish hostility toward the Alans, which apparently originated with the Alan's victory in 406, was probably fostered to some extent by Childeric's efforts to seize the Alan capital of Orléans and by Clovis's raids into Armorica. Childebert I's imprisonment of Count Alan Judual and his support of the foreign usurper Conomor suggest a further division between the Armoricans (Alan and Celt alike) and the Franks. The wars carried on by later Armorican leaders against the Merovingians and Carolingians only seem to reinforce the theme of Armorican-Frankish hostility.[19]

Alan victories were ignored by pro-Frankish chroniclers like Fredegar and the author of the *Liber Historiae Francorum*, and the latter even went so far as to turn Frankish defeats into victories. Early in the eighth century the author of the *Liber* presented his version of the Trojan origin of the Franks. After the fall of Troy the princes led their bands of followers into Europe. Aeneas, who is characterized as a tryant, led his followers to Italy, while Priam and Antenor, the ancestors of the Franks, went to Pannonia. There, according to the *Liber,* the Franks encountered the Alans who are characterized as "perverse" and "rotten." The Alans are said to have revolted against the Roman Emperor Valentinian who defeated them and drove them beyond the Danube into the Moesian Swamps. Valentinian then promised the Franks a valuable gift if they would finish off the Alans. This they are alleged to have done in a brave and bloody manner. Thus, the Frankish chronicler avenged a real Frankish defeat

18. *Lex Salica, 100 Titel-Text*, pp. 82–84, 86–90.
19. Chadwick, *Early Brittany*, pp. 225–237, for the later period. For continued Alan-Frankish contact in the east of Gaul in the later fifth and early sixth centuries, see n. 45 below.

at the hands of the Alans by creating an imaginary Frankish victory over the Alans.[20]

Yet another genealogy, this one probably from the later sixth or early seventh century, provides additional evidence that the Alans, like the Franks, sought aggrandizement through literary means. This genealogy purports to list the Roman rulers in Gaul during the second half of the fifth century: "Primus rex Romanorum Allanius dictus est. Allanius genuit Pabolum. Pabolus Egetium. Egetius genuit Egegium. Egegius genuit Siagrium per quem Romani regnum perdiderunt."[21]

The last mentioned ruler, Syagrius, was defeated by Clovis in 486 and murdered soon after that. He had succeeded his father, Aegidius, who died about 464. Aegidius seems to be represented in this text by either Egetius or Egegius. It is possible that the writer who composed the genealogy listed two men for one, i.e., Aegidius was divided into two persons, Egetius and Egegius. It is also possible and more probable that one of the names above was intended to represent Aetius, the Roman commander in Gaul who defeated Attila at Châlons in 451, and the other name was meant to represent Syagrius's father. Pabolus seems to be a corruption of Paulus, the Roman *comes* who commanded imperial forces in Armorica from about 460 to 470. The inclusion of Alanus (Allanius) seems to be another attempt to glorify the *Alani* who flourished in Armorica, supported the Roman cause, and helped to defeat the Huns in 451 and the Visigoths in 507.[22]

The assimilation of the Alans into the Celtic-dominated culture of Armorica was a reciprocal process. In the area of military tactics the Alans, who along with other steppe peoples exercised a profound influence on Roman cavalry development, were of great importance in the development of Armorican cavalry. During the later Roman empire as in earlier times, the Celts, whether Briton or Breton, enjoyed no reputation at all as horsemen, though classical authors did note their prowess in the field of chariotry. Pro-

20. *LHF*, chs. 2, 3.
21. G. Kurth, *Histoire poétique des mérovingiens* (Paris, 1893), pp. 87, 96, 517–523. The text is found on p. 521.
22. Bachrach, "Alites," p. 35.

copius, writing toward the middle of the sixth century, repeated an old story, which he apparently believed and which he expected his audience to believe, to the effect that there were no horses in Britain. Thus the inhabitants, upon visiting other places, were said not to know the simplest things about horsemanship such as mounting, much less anything about riding itself.[23]

By the twelfth century, however, the reputation of Armorican horsemen was exactly the opposite from what it had been in ancient times. In approximately 1120 Stephen of Llandaff, the author of the *Life of Saint Teilo* (a Welsh saint of the early sixth century with close Armorican connections), tells how the saint prayed to the Lord that the Armoricans would become the best horsemen in the world. The author goes on to say that Teilo's prayers were answered and that even today (that is, ca. 1120) the Armoricans are seven times more effective on horseback than on foot. Geoffrey of Monmouth, a contemporary of Stephen who also harbored a pro-Armorican bias, describes a battle, alleged to have taken place in the late fifth century, in which a detachment of Armorican horsemen saved the day for Ambrosius Aurelianus.[24]

Though Stephen's account of St. Teilo and Geoffrey's *Historia* contain much that is accurate and useful about Armorican history in the early Middle Ages, it is uncertain whether these authors were relying upon an ancient tradition for their glorification of Breton cavalry in the late fifth and early sixth centuries or merely

23. F. Lot, "Migrations saxonnes en Gaule et en Grande-Bretagne," *RH*, CXIX (1915), 34, and "La conquête du pays d'entre Seine-et-Loire par les Francs," *RH*, CLXIV (1930), 246.

24. *Liber Landavensis*, pp. 106–107: "et coram omni populo Sanctus Teliaus Episcopus rogavit Deum, et imprecatus et suppliciter, ut milites Armorici fortiores fierent in equitando omnibus gentibus, ut inde patriam suam tuerentur, et victoriose se de inimicis suis ulciscerentur. Et illud Privilegium quod Sanctus Telaus impetravit a Domino sibi collatum, usque hodie permanent inibi secundum testimonia et commentaria omnium illius patriae seniorum. Sunt enim Armorici amplius victoriosi in equitando, septies quam ut essent pedites." On this see also Joseph Loth, "La vie de Saint Teliau," *Annales de Bretagne*, IX (1893), 80–85, and Edmund Faral, *La légende arthurienne*, II (Paris, 1929), 236–237. Geoffrey, *Hist.*, VI, 121: "Tria milia ex Armoricanis jussit equis adesse, ceteros cum insulanis mixtim in acies constituit." See also Bachrach, "Armorican Chivalry," p. 166.

repeating contemporary feelings about the prowess of Armorican horsemen and creating historical evidence for their conclusions. In either case, however, both of these twelfth-century writers indicate a substantial Armorican reputation for horsemanship which was the very opposite of the ancient tradition. Stephen's dubious explanation for the origins of Armorican equestrian prowess suggests strongly that more mundane influences were at work.

Armorican horsemen were thought significant long before the twelfth century. Regino of Prüm in the tenth century, Hermoldus Nigellus and Nithard in the ninth century, and Gregory of Tours in the sixth century take note of Breton horsemen. The virtual absence of such accounts in the seventh and eighth centuries seems to be the result of the comparative lack of detailed narrative sources during this era and of the effectual separation of Brittany from the mainstream of late Merovingian and early Carolingian history, upon which the jejune sources focus.[25]

To seek the origins of Armorican chivalry it is perhaps not unreasonable to go back to the Alans who were being assimilated into Breton society by the early sixth century if not earlier. Incidentally, this is the period which is pointed to by Stephen of Llandaff and corroborated by Geoffrey of Monmouth as the time when Armorican cavalry developed.

As already noted, the Alans' military tactics resembled those of the Huns who "enter battle drawn up in wedge-shaped masses, while their medley of voices makes a savage noise. And as they are lightly equipped for swift motion, and unexpected action, they purposely divide suddenly into scattered bands and attack, rushing about in disorder here and there, dealing terrific slaughter; and because of their extraordinary rapidity of movement . . . they fight from a distance with missiles . . . they gallop over the intervening spaces and fight hand to hand with swords."[26]

The Alans, too, raised a terrifying yell when they charged into

25. Regino, *Chron.*, A.D. 889; Hermoldus, *Poème*, III, 1628ff; Nithard, *Hist.*, III, 6; Gregory, *G.M.*, ch. 60.
26. Ammianus Marcellinus, XXXI, 2, 9.

battle, and they also utilized the mounted phalanx on occasion. Like the Huns, the Alans disdained fighting on foot, and, as has been mentioned, they actually regarded even going on foot as somehow debasing. Isidore of Seville points out that the Alans were essentially useless militarily without their horses. The Alans were mobile in their military tactics; but, unlike the Huns, the Alans who settled in Armorica utilized armor for both themselves and their mounts.[27]

This description of Alan horsemen thus gleaned from the writings of Ammianus Marcellinus and several later commentators who speak of the Alans' military customs bears a marked resemblance to the Armorican horsemen described by Hermoldus Nigellus during the first half of the ninth century. Hermoldus's Bretons fight on horseback, wear armor as do their horses, and hurl javelins at their enemies.[28] Perhaps the most interesting bit of evidence is provided by Regino of Prüm who, in the tenth century, indicated in passing that the Bretons fight like the Hungarian cavalry. The Bretons do not push their attack home but swerve their horses after each attack, and they differ from the Magyars only in that the latter shoot arrows, while the former hurl javelins. The Magyars, it should be further noted, did not dismount to fight on foot.[29] What seems significant, however,

27. *Ibid.*, XXXI, 2, 21; Claudian, *De Cons. Stilic.*, XXX, 109; Isidore, *Etym.*, XIX, 23, 7: "sine equis inertes extant Alani . . . " Bachrach, "Armorican Chivalry," pp. 167–168.
28. Hermoldus, *Poème*, III, 1494, 1659, 1706, and esp. 1628ff: "Armat equum, semet, fidos armatque sodales,/ Ambas missilibus armat et ipse manus,/ Scandit equum velox, stimulis praefigit acutis/ Frena tenens; giros dat quadrupes varios."
29. Regino, *Chron.*, A.D. 889, compares the Hungarians to the Scythians as described by Justin, who wrote in the second century A.D. Regino also notes the similarity of the Bretons to the Hungarians. By implication, however, he also compares the Bretons to the Scythians. This in a sense provides a complete circle: the Scythians, Alans, and Huns, all steppe peoples, have very similar military tactics. Regino links the Hungarians to the Scythians and the Bretons to the Hungarians. Here an attempt is being made to link the Bretons to the Alans, who as steppe people may be connected with the Scythians. Copying from Justin, Regino writes, "Pugnant aut procurrentibus equis aut terga dontibus, saepe etiam fugam simulant. Nec pugnare diu possunt: ceterum intolerandi forent, si quantus est impetus, vis tanta et perserverantia esset. Plerumque in ipso ardore certaminis prelia deserunt ac paulo post pugnam ex fuga repetunt, ut cum maxime vicisse

is that the Alan element in Breton society could have had so long-lasting a military influence; more than four centuries after the initial settlement the Alano-Breton horsemen of Armorica sufficiently resembled their erstwhile steppe brethren to suggest a comparison to at least one contemporary.

In seeking the origins of Armorican chivalry, two points are worth emphasizing. First of all Regino's observations on the similarity between the military tactics of the Bretons and those of the Magyars imply that steppe influences were present in the Breton's military tactics. Before the end of the fifth century Alans settled in Armorica were being assimilated by their non-equestrian neighbors. Secondly, it seems reasonable to assume that if Regino rightly detected steppe tactics among the Bretons, then these tactics were of Alan origin since there were no other steppe settlers in early medieval Armorica.

The Alans disliked fighting on foot and at least two other steppe peoples, the Huns and the Sarmatians, shared this attitude. Both these peoples were kept from fighting on foot by technical difficulties. The Huns are said to have had inadequate shoes, while the Sarmatians were burdened with such heavy armor that they could not maneuver on foot. It may be said that the similarity between the Alans and the Huns or the Sarmatians may have extended only to inadequate shoes or heavy armor, but no conclusion on this detail can be more than conjecture. It is clear, however, that the Alans were against fighting on foot either because of technology or because of ideology.[30]

In a recent work Warren Hollister has written that "in every important battle of the Anglo-Norman age, the bulk of the feudal cavalry dismounted to fight. At Tinchebrai, in 1106, an eyewitness account reports that 96 per cent of King Henry's army was on foot, including the king himself and all his barons. In 1119 a high

te putes, tunc tibi discrimen subeundum sit." Then Regino adds, "Quorum pugna, quo ceteris gentibus inusitata, eo et periculosior. Iter horum et Brittonum conflictum hos unum interest, quo illi missilibus, isti sagittis utuntur."

30. Ammianus Marcellinus, XXXI, 2, 6, and Tacitus, *Hist.*, I, 79, for the Huns and Sarmatians, respectively.

A History of the Alans

percentage of King Henry's force at Brémule was made up of dismounted knights, and according to one contemporary, the battle was won by a charge of closely packed infantry. At Bourg Théroulde (1124), most of the Anglo-Norman knights again fought on foot, and at Northallerton (1138), they dismounted to a man. . . . At Lincoln (1141) the king and his knights again dismounted and fought as infantry."[31]

Did the Bretons conform to the tactics of their Anglo-Norman neighbors or did the Alan bias against dismounted combat persist? It is likely that Regino of Prüm would not have noted the similarity in tactics between the Bretons and the Magyars if the former had readily dismounted and fought on foot.[32] In the Anglo-Norman era Breton horsemen took part in two battles concerning which there is sufficient information for us to compare their tactics with those of their contemporaries. At Tinchebrai, where 96 per cent of Henry's army fought on foot, the king ordered the Breton cavalry to remain mounted along with the men of Maine. At Lincoln, where the king and most of his cavalry dismounted, the Bretons did not do so. Although the Breton horsemen retreated at Lincoln, it is more plausible that they were able to withdraw because they were mounted rather than that they remained mounted so they could desert.[33] During the early seventh century, Isidore of Seville commented that the Alans were militarily ineffective on foot; five centuries later Stephen of Llandaff similarly noted that the Armoricans were seven times more effective on horseback than on foot. These observations, if accurate, suggest why the Bretons were ordered to remain mounted while their Anglo-Norman contemporaries dismounted and fought on foot. Two examples (Tinchebrai and Lincoln) are surely not conclusive, but taken with the remarks by Isidore, Regino, and

31. Warren Hollister, *Anglo-Saxon Military Institutions* (Oxford, 1962), pp. 131–132.
32. See two articles by Karl Leyser in which Magyar and Breton tactics are discussed: "The Battle of Lech," *History*, L (1965), 1–25; and "Henry I and the Beginnings of the Saxon Empire," *EHR*, LXXXIII (1968), 17–18.
33. For Tinchebrai, see Charles W. David, *Robert Curthose* (Cambridge, Mass., 1920), pp. 245ff; for Lincoln, see John Beeler, *Warfare in England, 1066–1189* (Ithaca, N.Y., 1966), pp. 114ff.

90

Stephen and viewed in relation to the small number of available sources, they do seem to indicate that the Bretons did not dismount to fight on foot as did their Anglo-Norman contemporaries.

From the Bayeux Tapestry it can be seen that in the late eleventh century the Normans and Bretons were armed in the same manner.[34] This suggests that no technical differences in arms and armor account for what seems to have been a difference in tactics between the Normans and Bretons. If it is valid to trace the origin of Breton chivalry to the Alans, then the Breton equestrian tradition is far older than that of either the Normans or the English, who are descended from the Vikings and the Anglo-Saxons, respectively. Several hundred years of mounted training, however, made the Normans quite adequate horsemen. Rather than viewing the Bretons as superior horsemen, should we not, perhaps, view them as inferior infantrymen? Since no technical differences are readily discernible between the arms and armor of the Normans and those of the Bretons, may it not be that the latter harbored some traditional bias against fighting on foot, an attitude which may have persisted from the fifth century?

An additional Alan influence upon the tactical repertoire of the fighting forces in western France was the feigned retreat. As mentioned earlier, the feigned retreat was a well-developed tactic of the steppe peoples. Arrian, Hadrian's legate in Cappadocia, noted in his work *Contra Alanos* that the Alans were adroit in the use of the feigned retreat; he goes on to give very specific instructions for the deployment of troops to defend against this tactic. Alans fighting in Roman service in northern Italy early in the fifth century appear to have used the feigned retreat tactic against the Visigoths. During the ninth century, Armorican horsemen frequently employed the feigned retreat. Regino of Prüm, who compared the tactics of the Bretons with those of the Magyars, was well aware that the Magyars were formidable in

34. *Bayeux Tapestry*, gen. ed. Sir Frank Stenton (London, 1957), pls. 63, 66. See also Beeler, *Warfare*, p. 19, n. 53, n. 54.

the use of the feigned retreat and he commented that the Bretons used it as well.[35]

At the battle of Hastings the feigned retreat was utilized effectively by the Normans and their Breton allies. William of Poitiers writes, "The Normans and their allies, observing that they could not overcome an enemy which was so numerous and so solidly drawn up, without severe losses, retreated, simulating flight as a trick. . . . [A]mong the barbarians there was great joy. . . . [S]ome thousands of them . . . threw themselves in pursuit of those whom they believed to be in flight. Suddenly the Normans reined in their horses, intercepted and surrounded the enemy, and killed them to the last man."[36] William of Malmesbury is more succinct: "The English . . . formed an impenetrable body, which would have kept them safe that day, if the Normans had not tricked them into opening their ranks by a feigned retreat."[37]

These accounts apply to the second retreat at Hastings. William of Poitiers, however, indicates that "twice the same trick was used." The first time the retreat was carried out by the Bretons under Count Alanus, who after the battle was singled out for his conspicuous role in the fray.[38]

In light of the extensive nature of Alan influence in Armorica, it can be expected that the feigned retreat tactic would have become part of the tactical repertoire of western France. It is hardly surprising that the Normans, who were very willing to adopt new and effective military techniques, learned to use the feigned retreat as well. In fact, within little more than a decade during the mid-eleventh century, the Normans used the feigned retreat at least three times: at Messina in 1053, at Arques (Normandy) in 1060, and at Hastings in 1066. The crusaders, fighting toward the

35. For the frequent use of the feigned retreat by Armorican horsemen, see Leyser, "Saxon Empire," pp. 17–18.
36. William of Poitiers, *Gesta Guillelmi*, II, 20.
37. William of Malmesbury, *De Gestis Regum Anglorum*, bk. III, 242. Other mentions of the feigned retreat at Hastings are found in Wace, ll. 8200ff, and *Chron. Monast. de Bello*, A.D. 1066.
38. *Gesta Guillelmi*, II, 21, and Geffrei Gaimar, *L'Estoire des Engleis*, ll. 5309ff, for the effective role played by Count Alan.

end of the eleventh century, used the feigned retreat as did their Turkish enemies from central Asia.[39]

THE ALANS IN SOUTHERN GAUL

The Alan settlements in the south of Gaul do not seem to have fared as well as those of Armorica. After having defected from their Visigothic allies in 414, these Alans were settled in the area between Toulouse and the Mediterranean. A few years later, however, the Visigoths, from whom these Alans had deserted, returned from Spain as imperial allies to dominate the southwest of Gaul. The Visigoths were Arian Christians and the Alan minority who lived among them were mostly pagans until the latter part of the fifth century, when they became orthodox Christians.[40]

The political and religious differences which divided the Alans and the Visigoths living in the south of Gaul perhaps help to account for the limited survival of Alan influence in that region as compared to the importance of Alan influence in Armorica. As already noted, the survival of Alan place names is an indication of this continuing influence in the south as well as in the north. In addition, during the early Middle Ages certain personal names like Alanus and Goar continued to be used in the area now under consideration. These names strongly suggest that the bearer was either of Alan descent or strongly influenced by some aspect of Alan culture.

One such person, whose name in the sources is spelled in various ways including Goeric and Goiaric, served the Visigothic King Alaric II who ruled at Toulouse. Goeric held the title of *vir illustris* and was given charge by Alaric of arranging for the drawing up of a law code for the Roman inhabitants of the Visigothic kingdom. It seems eminently reasonable that Alaric would have chosen an orthodox Christian of Alan origin to deal with the Roman lawyers and perhaps with the clergy in working out a law code for the Visigoths' Roman subjects. The Alans of this area had a long history of cooperation with the Romans, and

39. Bachrach, "Feigned Retreat," pp. 344–347.
40. See n. 3 above.

93

adherence to orthodox Christianity would strengthen any official's position vis-à-vis the Gallo-Romans. In fact, using orthodox Christians with strong ties to the empire for tasks which dealt with the "Roman" populations was standard procedure among the Franks, the Ostrogoths, and the Visigoths.[41]

Shortly after the publication of the law code for which Goeric was responsible, the Merovingian King Clovis, an orthodox Christian, led an army, including substantial numbers of Armorican Alans, into Aquitaine, conquered the Visigoth's Gallic lands, and killed Alaric II. In the wake of this disaster, Goeric was held prisoner by the new king, Gesalic, in the royal palace at Barcelona. Soon after, Gesalic had Goeric murdered.[42] It should be noted that other important orthodox Christians in Aquitaine who supported the Merovingian cause suffered at the hands of the Visigoths.[43]

A later contemporary of Goeric was St. Goar, *homo aquitanicus*, who was born in the south of Gaul during the reign of Clovis's son Childebert (d. 558). Goar's parents, as noted earlier, had Roman names but they remembered their Alan heritage by giving their son an Alan name. While probably still in his teens, Goar decided to take up the religious life and became a hermit. He journeyed to the Trier area, and there he built a little cell near the confluence of the Lochbach and the Rhine in the district today called Ober-Wesel.[44]

It might seem odd that a youth would wander several hundred miles from his home to become a recluse when there were many isolated places closer by where a committed individual could lead a perfectly respectable hermitic existence. Yet, there were during this period noteworthy political and religious connections be-

41. *Supp. Leg. Rom.* (ed. Zeumer), ch. 1: "domno Alarico rege ordinante viro inlustre Goiarico comite." See also *ibid.*, ch. 3; E. A. Thompson, *The Goths in Spain* (Oxford, 1969), pp. 114–115, 144; and *HGL*, I, 527–528.

42. *Chron. Caesaraug.*, s.a. 5101: "his coss. Gesalecus Goericum Barcinone in palatio interfecit." Thompson, *Goths in Spain*, pp. 8, 115, and *HGL*, I, 544.

43. Bachrach, *Merovingian Military Organization*, p. 7.

44. *V. Goar.*, ch. 1.

tween Aquitaine and eastern Gaul. In addition, the prospect of contact with some of the Alan settlements in the east of Gaul may have seemed attractive to a youth bearing such an obviously Alan name.[45]

The story given us in St. Goar's *Vita* is remarkably undramatic, and the only incident which might reflect his Alan heritage, even in a remote manner, concerns a charge of gluttony. It seems that Goar's reputation for piety attracted numerous pilgrims to his cell. (Could some of these visitors have been descendants of Alan settlers in eastern Gaul who were motivated by curiosity concerning Goar's name?) In any event, Goar made a point of providing those who visited him with a place to sleep and food to eat. Much to the consternation of the ecclesiastical officials in the area, Goar was well known to eat a hearty breakfast with his guests. He was therefore charged with gluttony and summoned to the bishop's court to defend himself. All this came about because by custom hermits were not permitted to eat before noon and in some cases not before sundown.[46]

Goar defended his eating breakfast with his guests first by arguing that the kingdom of God is to be found not in material things such as food, but in righteous peace and joy in the Holy Spirit. More importantly he contended that he was bound to provide the pilgrims who visited his cell with hospitality and that it would be inhospitable to serve them while abstaining himself. In this last point we see the articulation of a fundamental nomadic social custom. To take food with one's guests is to be hospitable; to fail to do so is to reserve your acceptance of them and thus to be inhospitable.[47]

Another Goar, this one recorded as Goeric in the texts, also pursued a career in both Aquitaine and eastern Gaul. This Goar

45. E. Ewig, "L'Aquitaine et les Pays Rhénans au haut moyen âge," *Cahiers de civilisation médiévale*, I (1958), 42–46. The Cosmographer of Ravenna, I, 26, writing in approximately 475–480, places a group of Alans in Gaul close to the Franks and Alamans. This was in the generation of Goar's parents.
46. *V. Goar.*, chs. 2–5.
47. *Ibid.*, chs. 6–7. For the hospitality customs of the nomads of the steppes, see Vernadsky, *Origins of Russia*, p. 12.

flourished during the first half of the seventh century, and his family seems to have been of some importance in the Albigeois. He served as count of Albi in 627; later his nephew Babo also held that position. Goeric's niece was the abbess of Troclar, a convent in the Albigeois. In 629 or 630, Goeric, who also bore the name Abbo, succeeded Arnulf as bishop of Metz. Thus, like St. Goar, his earlier namesake, Goeric traveled from Aquitaine to the east of Gaul to fulfill his religious destiny.[48]

This reliance upon little more than names to sustain a history of the Alans points up the paucity of the evidence and suggests the desirability of discussing some of the strengths and weaknesses of personal name evidence. In every case where a source mentions the ethnic background of some one named Goar he is said to be an Alan. In addition, it has been found that during the early Middle Ages no one bearing an Alan name in the West had come from a region not shown by other evidence to be an area of Alan settlement. Thus it seems reasonable to assume that someone bearing the name Goar during the early Middle Ages was either of Alan descent or was strongly influenced by some aspect of Alan culture through his neighbors.[49]

Working with the name Goar and its variant spellings which appear during the fifth, sixth, and seventh centuries presents an additional problem. The Latin Goar, occasionally Goarus, is found in the Greek sources as Γωαρ. These versions of the name, however, seem merely to be the classical rendition of the original Alan name approximated by the modern Ossetic Iæukhar. Through what seems to be Germanic traditions, Iæukhar emerges as Eochar, itself having many variant spellings.[50]

We learn about this dual nature of the name Iæukhar from the career of the Alan ruler of Orléanais who flourished during the first half of the fifth century. He is called both Goar and Eochar in various manuscripts, and this is done in a manner

48. V. Arnulfi, chs. 19, 23. HGL, I, 671.
49. See Krusch's remarks in his introduction to V. Goar., p. 405.
50. Ibid., and Vernadsky, "Eurasian Nomads," pp. 424–425. Cf. H. W. Bailey, "Iranian ARYA- and DAHA-," Transactions of the Philological Society (1959), p. 81.

which indicates that these were two versions of the same name. The texts make it clear that the particular chief in question had only one name which in turn had two separate renderings. It is reasonable that Iæukhar should have his name rendered in both a classical manner (Goar) and in a Germanic style (Eocharic) since he played an important role in early medieval Gaul where both Germans and Romans united to create a new, medieval culture.[51]

An analogy perhaps will clarify the matter. Let us presume that a German named Heinrich settled in Quebec, Canada, where he encountered both English-speaking Canadians and French Canadians. The latter would call him Henri while the former would just as probably speak of him as Henry. Among those of Heinrich's descendants who became a part of the French Canadian community there would be a tendency to honor their ancestor by naming their children Henri, and among the descendants who settled within the English-speaking community the inclination to name their children Henry would probably prevail.

Among the various spellings of Eochar for which there is firm evidence we find Eocharich and Eothar.[52] These variants would seem to cast some light on the background of the magnate Eutharic (Eotharic?) who married Amalasuentha, the daughter of Theodoric the Ostrogoth. Eutharic lived among the Visigoths, was an Arian Christian, and seems to have been a man of some consequence. According to the *Gesta Theodorici*, Eutharic was born *ex Alanorum stirpe*.[53] That an individual of Alan *stirps* could rise to a place of importance within the Visigothic kingdom was demonstrated by the *vir illustris* Goeric who supervised the drawing up of Alaric's Roman law code. Eutharic's Arianism

51. *V. Germani*, p. 271, and Vernadsky, "Eurasian Nomads," pp. 424–425.
52. *V. Germani*, p. 271.
53. *Gesta Theodorici*, ch. 13: "Amalsuindam, terciam filiam, Eutarico, ex Alanorum stirpe venienti, evocato ab Hispania tradidit." For further discussion of Eutharic, see Hodgkin, *Italy and Her Invaders*, III, 329ff. The efforts of Jordanes, *Getica*, ch. 58, to make Eutharic an Amal rather than an Alan is shown by Schmidt, *Deutsche Stämme*, I, 108–109, to be another of Jordanes's efforts to glorify the Goths.

was an additional asset in his marriage within the Ostrogothic royal family and may even have been the key to that particular success. His Arianism also suggests a greater degree of assimilation with the Visigoths than that enjoyed by the two men named Goar discussed above who were orthodox Christians. This in turn may help to explain why the Germanic version of the name Iæukhar prevailed over the classical version; it explains thus why he was Euthar and not Goar.

Important men bearing names of Alan provenance, as well as one man who is identified in a medieval source as being of Alan stock, played noteworthy roles in Aquitaine and among the Visigoths even after the fall of the Kingdom of Toulouse in 507–508. Two of those who flourished in Aquitaine also made their mark in the east of Gaul where there had been Alan settlements from the early fifth century. Unfortunately, there is no additional evidence to connect St. Goar who settled in the Trier area and Bishop Goeric of Metz with these settlements.

The survival of Alan influences in Spain was not, however, limited to a lone magnate named Eutharic. The Visigoths did, for example, adopt the feigned retreat tactic and used it successfully during the sixth century.[54] The continued existence of several Alan place names in Spain also suggests that Alan influence was not completely erased by Visigothic domination.[55] As late as 575 Orense, a part of Galicia where the Alans are known to have flourished with imperial support until about 428–429, was controlled by a *senior loci* with the very Alan-sounding name of Aspidius. The Asp- element derives from the Iranian word for horse as exemplified in the name of the famous East Roman Alan general Aspar. Aspidius may have been a Latinized form of the Iranian 'Ασπαδας or perhaps of the name 'Ασπισας as they appear in Greek form.[56]

54. Gregory, *Hist.*, IX, 31. Bachrach, "Feigned Retreat," p. 346.
55. See appendix III, nos. 19, 21, 22.
56. Thompson, *Goths in Spain*, p. 62. John Biclar, *Chron.*, s.a. 575: "Leovegildus rex Aregenses montes ingreditur, Aspidium loci seniorem cum uxore et filiis captivos ducit. . . ." For the name, see Ferdinand Justi, *Iranisches Namenbuch* (Marburg, 1895), pp. 45–46.

There seems to have been no sense of political solidarity among the descendants of these various groups; this, of course, is to be expected since their ancestors had none. While the Alans in their nomad days did have a sense of religious solidarity, this no longer existed after they came west. Thus, the influence of orthodox and Arian Christianity further fragmented the cultural unity of the Alans. Because of the vagaries of political fortune, Alans living under Visigothic control were of both orthodox and Arian persuasion. Some Alans in Spain seem to have served the Goths while others, like Aspidius and his followers, were destroyed by them.

CULTURAL INTERCHANGE

The links of political interaction between the various Alan settlements in the West are nonexistent, but there are vague hints of cultural interchange. From archaeological finds we are provided with a modicum of evidence which points to a cultural link between some of the areas of Alan settlement in Gaul. Aquitanian style ornamentation which has been identified as adorning some 134 artifacts, mostly belt buckles, from the later sixth and seventh centuries depicts central Asiatic motifs of Alan provenance. The two major find areas for these artifacts are the regions between Toulouse and the Mediterranean in southern Gaul and between Orléans and Blois and as far north as Saosnes (Sarthe) in Armorica. A third and much smaller find area is just to the north of Lake Geneva on the present Franco-Swiss border (see map 6, page 70).[57]

57. Nils Åberg, *The Occident and the Orient in the Art of the Seventh Century*, pt. III (Stockholm, 1947), pp. 40–69. Åberg's contention that the Aquitanian buckles "would have represented the same population as, during the time of the Gallic Visigothic Kingdom, were represented by the Aquitanian sarcophagi" leads him to argue that "the centre of gravity of the distribution lies in the area between Bordeaux and the Mediterranean" for both groups (p. 46). On the basis of the evidence presented by Ward Perkins (upon whom Åberg relies), "The Sculpture of Visigothic France," *Archaeologia*, LXXXVII (1938), 79–128, Åberg's conclusions seem unwarranted. The Aquitanian buckles are not found in northern Aquitaine (only six come from north of the Charente but south of Rouillé [Deux-Sèvres]). Of the 134 Aquitanian pieces, fifty-five are found between Toulouse and

There is general agreement that the Aquitanian style exhibits a mélange of many influences, including Frankish, Visigothic, Burgundian, and Coptic motifs. In addition, two aspects of Aquitanian style ornamentation derive their inspiration from central Asiatic sources: the four-footed animals depicted in plate 3, and the severely schematized human figures in plate 4. Nils Åberg, the scholar who first discovered the Aquitanian style, observes that the animals depicted here should not be confused with the lions and winged griffins characteristic of Burgundian art, and the schematized human figures with their squared shoulders, downward pointing arms, and bowed legs ought not to be confused with the orans Daniel figures often accompanied by a pair of animals. These latter motifs are also found frequently in Burgundian contexts. Both the Aquitanian style quadruped and the human figures generally appear on a dotted background.[58]

The central Asiatic nature of this animal ornamentation is attested by numerous parallels from Hungary during the "Hun" period and from south Russia. The Hungarian examples include backward-looking quadrupeds from Csúny, Nemesrölogy, and Dunapentele, and forward-looking quadrupeds from Szeged, Keszthely, and Regöly. From south Russia the Zmeiskii Tomb provides parallels for these animals as do finds from Kamunta (see plates 5a, b; 6; 7a, b).[59]

the Mediterranean and only seventeen between Toulouse and Bordeaux. This suggests that the former area, which has more than three times as many pieces, is the center of gravity for the style under discussion. Further, Åberg's effort to identify the buckle makers as the descendants of the sarcophagi makers ignores the Loire group among the former. Perkins does not show that the sarcophagi under discussion in his work had a center of production in the Orléanais or one north of Geneva.

The distribution of Aquitanian style artifacts depicted on map 6 is drawn from Åberg's map, p. 62. See Bernard S. Bachrach, "Two Alan Motifs in Åberg's Aquitanian Style," *Central Asiatic Journal*, XVI (1972), 81–94.

58. Åberg, *Occident*, pp. 42ff, and Bachrach, "Alan Motifs," pp. 83–84.

59. M. I. Rostovtzeff, "Le centre de l'Asie, la Russie, la Chine, et le style animal," *Skythika*, I (Prague, 1929), pls. 36, 37; Joseph Hampel, *Alterthümer des frühen Mittelalters in Ungarn* (Brunswick, 1905), pl. 97, fig. 2; pl. 162, fig. 3; and figs. 1946, 1970, 1971; V. A. Kusnetzov, "Alanskie Plemena Severnogo Kaukaza," *Materialy i issledovaniia po Arkheologii SSSR*, CVI (Moscow, 1962), pl. 11, figs. 1, 2, 4, 5, 8. E. Chantre, *Recherches anthropologiques dans le Caucase*, III (Paris, 1887), pl. 8.

South Russian parallels of the little schematized human figures are also found at Kamunta and Kiev (see plate 8). The last illustration in plate 8, which is from Kiev, is of special interest because its execution is considerably more sophisticated than either the Aquitanian pieces or the other Russian examples; thus it depicts even more graphically the central Asiatic horseman with his characteristically bowed legs. While the other pieces are more stylized, they all exhibit this motif which is indicative of central Asiatic equestrian life. Although this motif is easily interpreted, the meaning of the squared shoulders and downward pointing arms as pictured on the Alan finds from south Russia and on the Aquitanian style pieces has not as yet been ascertained. Nevertheless, they are very different, as Åberg has already pointed out, from the representations of human figures usually found in Gaul during this period, which are those in the orans position with their arms upraised.

Although the Aquitanian style exhibits many influences, none of the barbarian heirs of the Roman empire except the Alans inhabited all the major find areas. The Visigoths dominated the south of Aquitaine and ruled over the Alan settlements in the area between Toulouse and the Mediterranean. The Visigoths, however, had no settlements in the Orléanais. The Franks did not have any important settlements either in the Orléanais or in southern Aquitaine. The Burgundians dominated the area around Lake Geneva, but they had little influence west of the Rhone and none in the Orléanais. In short, the only consistent influence of a central Asiatic nature within the major find areas of Aquitanian style artifacts was that of the Alans and their descendants. That craftsmen working in areas of noteworthy Alan influence would incorporate central Asiatic motifs into their work seems reasonable; and equally reasonable is the overtly mélange nature of the Aquitanian style since Alan culture itself seems to have been in many ways overtly assimilative.

The belt buckles of the Aquitanian style are of the shield-on-tongue variety and thus are composed of three basic parts: the buckle loop, the shield, and the plaque, each of which is decorated in some manner. One such buckle loop, from which the shield and the plaque are missing, has an important inscription on it (see plate 9a). As can be seen, the buckle loop is oval in shape, which made it necessary to fit the letters into a curved form. In addition, the surface of the loop is curved rather than flat; this too increased the difficulty in cutting the inscription and probably caused its execution to be less than perfect (see plate 9b). I had the opportunity to study the buckle loop and the inscription at the museum in Vendôme during the summer of 1968 and suggest the following reading:

LAVAZ.TURC[us]

FLAVIGERASPUS[60]

The lower register of the description is the easier to decipher. I recommend that FLAVIGERASPUS be divided into two parts: FLAVI and GERASPUS, or more grammatically Flavius Geraspus. It was not uncommon for barbarians in the later sixth and seventh centuries to use the Roman name Flavius. Two examples are Flavius Recesuintus and Flavius Chintasuintus.[61] Although Recesuinth and Chindasuinth are good Visigothic names, we must look elsewhere for the provenance of Gerasp. The -asp element provides a clue to the origin of the name and can be identified as Iranian as in Aspar and Aspidius. A perusal of Justi's standard collection of Iranian names indicates that during ancient and medieval times Gersasp was a commonly used name among the peoples who spoke Iranian languages and those whom they influenced. The omission of an "s" from Gersasp to Gerasp in a primitive inscription which was cut thousands of

60. L. Franchet, "Une colonie Scytho-Alaine en Orléanais au V⁰ siècle," *Revue scientifique*, LXVIII (1930), 78, 109, figs. 13A and 20. The inscription as originally transcribed by Camille Jullian and communicated by letter to Franchet (cited in "Une colonie," pp. 109–110) has been followed in my interpretation except where Jullian reads "GIERUSPU." I have interpreted the three lines after the G as an E rather than as an IE which would seem to need four lines; and I have considered the < before the S to be an A rather than a U; and finally I have taken the snake-like figure following the U to be an S rather than a space filler.
61. See *Lex Visig.*, bk. VI, xii, xiii, for example. A. Mócsy, "Der Name Falvius als Rangbezeichnung in der Spätantike," *Akte IV Kongress für griechische und lateinische Epigraphik* (Vienna, 1964), pp. 257–263.

miles from the place of the name's origin and after almost two
and a half centuries of cultural interchange should not cause us
to reject the identicalness of the two names. Moreover, it should
be pointed out that though Gersasp was itself a popular name it
was already a corruption of Keresasp, indicating that even in the
steppe homeland and its environs names were not always rendered accurately all the time.[62]

(I have been unable to decipher the upper register of the inscription—LAVAZ.TURC[us]—in any way which represents more than
conjecture.)[63]

The cultural interchange between the major Alan settlement
areas in Gaul which is suggested by the distribution of Aquitanian style artifacts is given additional substance by the story of
St. Alan. The town of Lavaur (Tarn) is located in the midst of
the southern Aquitanian style artifact find area. Local tradition
in the area of Lavaur maintains that a St. Alan came there to
preach and eventually built a monastery. In addition, medieval
records have survived of six churches in the area, including the
cathedral of Lavaur, which were dedicated to St. Alan. The town
of Algans is only ten miles south of Lavaur, and the town of Alos
(medieval *Alanus*), a few miles from Lavaur, is said to have
been the site of the church and monastery complex built by St.
Alan. A tenth-century charter tells us that an *ecclesia Alani* at
Alos was in ruins and deserted by the monks. The charter also
maintains that the ruined buildings with their appurtenances
were conveyed by their possessor, a certain Deda, to the monastery of Conques in the Albigeois (see map 6).[64]

62. Justi, *Iranisches Namenbuch*, pp. 114, 161–162.

63. It is possible that the TURC[us] element is an abbreviated form of
TURCILINGUS. The *Turcilingi* were a minor Germanic tribe which flourished
during the fifth century (Schmidt, *Deutsche Stämme*, I, 349–350), and
some of its members may have settled in the Orléanais during the mid-fifth
century (Reynolds and Lopez, "Odoacer," pp. 39ff).

64. Emile Jolibois, "Aquelle epoque vivait St. Alain?" *Revue historique,
scientifique et littéraire du département du Tarn*, I (1877), 141–142,
154–155, 183–186. See also Edmond Cabié, "Alos en Albigeois aux Xe et
XIe siècles," *Revue historique, scientifique et littéraire du département du
Tarn*, XXIII (1926), 122–129; HGL, I, 709–710. *Cart. de Conques*, pp.
lxix, lxxi, and nos. 302, 480. See appendix III, nos. 27 and 43.

Though St. Alan is said to have flourished in the Lavaur area during the latter part of the seventh century, a church which by the tenth century was already in ruins and had been in that state since the memory runneth not counter could possibly have been built some 250 years earlier and have been the work of the holy man under discussion. The seventh-century date for St. Alan's *floruit* is based largely upon his *Vita* which in fact was probably not his *Vita* at all but an interpolated version of the *Life of St. Amand*, the patron saint of Belgium. It seems that a monk working in Aquitaine appropriated that part of St. Amand's *Vita* which deals with his adventures in the south of Aquitaine and introduced some substitutions. In particular, St. Amand's foundation of the monastery of Nant in the Rouergue in approximately 660 is used by the author of the *Vita S. Alani*, who substitutes Lavaur for Nant and King Sigibert, who is credited with confirming the monastery at Lavaur, for King Childeric, who is alleged to have confirmed the foundation of Nant.[65]

Although the use of another saint's *Vita* does not automatically disqualify the evidence presented in the new version, it certainly places its truth in doubt. More importantly, however, is the introduction of St. Amand into the problem of Alan, since this provides a link between the south of Gaul and Armorica. Amand was born at Herbauges near Nantes. After leaving his home, much against the wishes of his father who was a very wealthy man, Amand visited for various periods of time at Oye near La Rochelle, Tours, and Bourges. He then went to Rome, preached in Belgic Gaul and among the Slavs. After returning to Gaul once again, he was exiled to Aquitaine by King Dagobert; there he preached in the lands of King Charibert II. Later Amand went back to Paris and then to Orléans. He became bishop of Maastricht and also preached to the Basques in Gascony. Amand's wide travels and even wider reputation made him very popular even in his own time. The many places named for St. Amand as well

65. *HGL*, I, 709–710, and Jolibois, "St. Alain," pp. 142, 183–185. Bouquet, III, 535: "S. Alanus impetravit à Rege Sigeberto locum unum in Gallia, qui dicitur Vaurum, et ibi Caenobium aedificavit. Sed Epsicopus proximae civitatis hoc molestè ferens, jussit famulis suis ut inde eum ejicerent, aut certè occiderent."

as the numerous manuscript copies of the various versions of his *Vita*, which were composed during the early Middle Ages, attest to this popularity.[66] Thus it would hardly have been unnatural for a monk, perhaps attached to the *ecclesia Alani* near Lavaur, to have made some useful changes in an easily available work for the purpose of giving greater support to the claims of his own house. The facts may have indeed been true; only the vehicle chosen to convey the facts was spurious.

Thus far the evidence has been examined in light of the probability that there really was a St. Alanus. More than one saint, however, has been created for some purpose or other and subsequently has had the acts of a real person attributed to him. Such might well have been the case at Lavaur, and the different dates upon which St. Amand and St. Alan are venerated, February 6 and November 26 respectively, do not prove the existence of the latter. It only proves that people revere what they believe to have been a saint who died on November 26.[67]

The puzzle of St. Alan, patron of Lavaur, is further compounded by the traditions relating to St. Alan, patron of Corlai. The latter *Alanus*, who is said to have been a wandering bishop, just like Alan of Lavaur, preached in Armorica, and his relics were located throughout the Middle Ages in a church in Quimper. He is venerated on November 27. Although Alan of Corlai is said to have visited the British Isles and Celtic tradition attributes to him several successful sons, the fact that his deeds are also associated with those of St. Amand is of particular interest.[68]

Two apparently separate traditions, one in the south of France and the other in Armorica, developed concerning a St. Alanus who flourished during the seventh century. The dates upon which both are honored, November 26 and 27, suggest that these two traditions may have more in common than the sharing of the

66. G. Deric, *Histoire ecclésiastique de Bretagne*, II (Saint-Brieuc, 1847), 125–127; Edouard de Moreau, *Saint Amand* (Louvain, 1927).
67. Jolibois, "St. Alain," p. 184.
68. Guy Lobineau, *Les vies de Saints de Bretagne*, I (Paris, 1886), xl; J. Loth, *Les noms des Saints Bretons* (Paris, 1910), p. 8; Rice Rees, *An Essay on the Welsh Saints* (London, 1836), p. 221; and Jolibois, "St. Alain," p. 185.

deeds of St. Amand, who is honored on February 6. Many unanswerable questions arise. Was there a wandering bishop named Alanus who visited Lavaur and Corlai? Were there two such bishops or only one? Was St. Amand, whose deeds are well documented, the bearer of another name, Alanus? And, in areas of Alan influence was he known by that alternate name? Finally, were the various St. Alans merely the creations of antiquarian monks in the early Middle Ages? In this last context it should be remembered that during the seventh century genealogies were created in Armorica by a monk of Alan descent to glorify his people just at the time when they were being assimilated by the numerically dominant non-Alan population of the area. Whatever the true explanation for St. Alan of Lavaur and St. Alan of Corlai, one or two, real or imaginary, the very existence and survival of their legends from the seventh century on tend to demonstrate the strength of Alan influence in the two major areas of Alan settlement during the early Middle Ages. These stories may even illustrate a degree of cultural interaction between the Alan settlements in Armorica and those in southern Gaul.

In Armorica where people still spoke the Alan language in the sixth century, Alan influences survived throughout the early Middle Ages. These influences can be seen in the dominance of Alan cavalry tactics, the creation of a cult devoted to St. Alanus with the naming of towns in his honor,[69] the compilation of genealogies in which Alanus is given a preeminent role, the survival of place names, and the prominence of certain personal names. With all this, however, the Alan element in the historical development of Armorica was relatively slight. In the westernmost areas, Celtic influences prevailed, while in the more eastern reaches of Armorica, Roman influence tended to dominate.

The ultimate importance in the Middle Ages of both Celtic and Latin influences should not, however, obscure the fact that Armorica was an area of cultural mixing not only where Celtic and Latin elements thrived but where German and Alan influences were also felt. Within this context, it is illuminating to re-

69. See appendix III, no. 47.

member the mélange nature of the Aquitanian style which included Germanic motifs of various types as well as Alan and Coptic influences. The idea of a mélange of influences, which seems so natural in artistic work, is more difficult to comprehend when focused upon a phenomenon like personal names. It is true that we find an Alan Judual, a count with two names, one Celtic and the other Alan, but he seems to have been an exception. The name *Alanus* itself has been challenged by those who have studied Armorican history from an essentially Celtic point of view. Thus the eighteenth-century historian Dom Lobineau contended that the name Alain, which is so popular in Breton history, may be derived from an ancient Breton word for foreigner—**Allan*. This explanation, however, has not gained acceptance, and modern scholars have abandoned the effort to provide a Celtic origin for *Alanus* by simply ignoring the question. The consensus of scholarly thought among early medievalists on this point is that Alain and its variants are derived from the central Asiatic *Alani*.[70]

Be that as it may, the question still must be asked, what ap-

70. Guy Lobineau, *Histoire de Bretagne*, II (Paris, 1707), col. 1771. For the consensus on the origin of Alanus, see A. Longnon, *Les noms de lieux de la France* (Paris, 1920), p. 133; A. Dauzat and Ch. Rostaing, *Dictionnaire etymologique des noms de lieux en France* (Paris, 1963), p. 8; A. Dauzat, *La toponymie française* (Paris, 1939), pp. 18, 48–50, 248; André Rolland de Denus, *Dictionnaire des appellation ethniques de la France et Colonies* (Paris, 1889), col. 9. Some scholars have argued that too many of these names have been ascribed to the *Alani* and more should be derived from the hypothetical Germanic name Allo or Allin. On this see Gröhler, *Ursprung*, II, 295, but cf. Gröhler, p. 7, and Marie-Therese Morlet, *Toponymie de la Thierache* (Paris, 1967), p. 51.

Jackson, *Language*, does not raise the question that *Alanus* might be of Celtic origin. The Celtic *Alauni* whom Ptolemy confuses with the *Alani* might be suggested as the basis for the popularity of the name Alain in Brittany. This, however, can be shown to be without foundation since wherever we find Alauna (the usual place name derived from the *Alauni*), we find the later Latin Alona and the French Allones or some variant. This is because the au dipthong becomes ō and not a. On this, see Jackson, *Language*, pp. 37, 306, 309, 313. A. Bournatzeff, "Noms toponymiques des lieux historiques en France," *Oss-Alains*, I (1953), 21–22, argues mistakenly that Allone and its variants derive from the plural of the Alan name for themselves, Iron. Chadwick, *Early Brittany*, pp. 150, 152–153, discusses the Alans in Armorica during the mid-fifth century but then ignores them thereafter. For the earliest use of the name *Alanus* as a personal name, see Jordanes, *Getica*, ch. 50.

proach is to be taken, when two peoples dwelling in the same general geographical area each have words which could equally be accounted as the basis of a particular name? Names, for example, with the element Cad- are very common in Celtic areas, and rightly so, since it is the Celtic root for the word *warrior*. Yet within the Indo-Iranian language group of which the Alan language is a part, the root Cad- means magnate or perhaps noble. Since the Celtic population in Armorica was undoubtedly much greater numerically than the Alan population, it would seem, on a statistical basis at least, that the vast majority of names containing a Cad- element owe their origin to Celtic influence; even in the fifth, sixth, and seventh centuries when Celtic influence had yet to reach the dominance it did later in the Middle Ages and Alan influence was much greater than it was to be in later times, the Celts still most surely outweighed the Alans in importance. Yet the statistical argument does not ensure that any particular name among the many hundreds which contain a Cad-element is of Celtic rather than of Alan provenance.[71]

For example, in the large area of central Armorica, which came under the control of Conomor toward the middle of the sixth century, there was a petty magnate named Caduon. We know little about him except his name—a name, incidentally, which not only contains the Cad- element that in the Alan language means magnate, an apt description of the man himself, but a name which was very similar to that of the Scythian chief Καδουιάς.[72]

This has not been meant as an argument that Caduon is of Alan descent or even that his name is of Alan provenance. The point has been raised to question the common practice of assuming that all names containing a Cad- element in early medieval Armorica may without question be classified as Celtic. And further, if such a hallowed convention is open even to the slightest doubt, are not some of the more controversial attributions of lit-

71. On the concept of cultural mixing, see Slicher van Bath, "Dutch Tribal Problems," pp. 319–338.
72. Justi, *Iranisches Namenbuch*, pp. 151, 498; Chadwick, "Colonization," p. 298.

erary and folklore themes also open to investigation as to their possible central Asiatic provenance or their having been influenced by the Alans and their descendants through a process of cultural interaction?

In this vein, let us look very briefly at some of the Arthurian material which plays such an important role in the legends and literature of medieval Armorica. It seems to be generally agreed today that a military commander of noteworthy talent flourished in Britain about 500 and stemmed the Saxon conquest for a time. During the early Middle Ages, this man—tradition calls him Arthur—was known in Wales, Cornwall, and Armorica. Bits and pieces of information survive suggesting that stories grew up around the historical Arthur which were less than true. Yet there is probably insufficient evidence to prove the existence of "a largely developed Arthur-saga" before Geoffrey of Monmouth published his *Historia Regum Britanniae* in approximately 1136. Geoffrey incorporated into this work some of the information which we know was circulating about Arthur in the early Middle Ages. He also probably included material about Arthur garnered from early sources of which no pre-Geoffrey record has survived. In addition, post-Geoffrey writers about Arthur may have culled bits and pieces of Arthuriana that were known from earlier times but which were ignored by Geoffrey and that left no other record except for the late romance in which it is found.[73]

It was shown earlier that Alan influence in Armorica was important during the early Middle Ages and particularly during the period in which Arthur flourished and his exploits gained some popularity; nevertheless, it remains to be seen if the Alans or their descendants may have influenced the Arthurian stories.

73. The bibliography of scholarly works on Arthuriana is truly immense, and no attempt will be made here to provide references to all the many positions that have been elaborated concerning the fine points which literary critics have thought worthy of debate. For easy access to many important arguments and the relevant bibliography, see *Arthurian Literature in the Middle Ages*, ed. R. S. Loomis (Oxford, 1959), and J. S. P. Tatlock, *The Legendary History of Britain* (Berkeley, 1950). Hanning, *The Vision of History*, provides some interesting insights into the intellectual milieu in which the Arthurian materials developed.

Perhaps Arthur is most famous for his magic sword Excalibur, Caliburn in Geoffrey's account. The hero's sword in medieval literature is very common, however; there is Beowulf's Naegling, Roland's Durendal, and Charlemagne's Joyeuse. The origin of Arthur's sword perhaps can be traced back to the eleventh-century Welsh poem *The Spoils of Annwfu*, where the weapon is carried off from the "otherworld" and probably given to Arthur. In a slightly later Welsh work, *Culhwch and Olwen*, Arthur appears with the sword Caledvwch.[74]

Some have argued that Caledvwch in *Culhwch* and Caliburn in Geoffrey's *Historia* have some connection with an Irish hero's sword called Caladbolg. Yet in tracing hero's swords it seems unwise to omit an early element in the development of the Charlemagne legend, Notker's *Gesta Karoli*, a work of the later ninth century. In the *Gesta*, Charles is pictured in an heroic posture: ". . . crested with an iron helmet, wearing iron gauntlets, . . . protected by an iron breastplate, an iron spear was held high in his left hand, for his right always rested on his unconquered sword."[75] Although a catalogue of martial accouterments may remind the reader of Arthur's weapons popularized by both *Culhwch* and Geoffrey's *Historia*, it is the sword which merits special attention in this context. Notker writes concerning it: "Nam dextra ad invictum calibem semper erat extenta." The context makes it clear that *calibs* is a sword, and its philological similarity to Arthur's Caliburn is remarkable.[76]

Arthur's sword is associated with various themes in the numerous stories in which it appears. The sword in the stone, for ex-

74. Tatlock, *Legendary History*, p. 202, and K. H. Jackson, "Arthur in Early Welsh Verse," in *Arthurian Literature*, pp. 15–17.
75. Notker, *Gesta Karoli*, II, 17: "Tunc visus est ipse ferreus Karolus ferrea galea cristatus, ferreis manicis armillatus, ferrea torace ferreum pectus humerosque Platonicos tutatus; hasta ferrea in altum subrecta sinistram impletus. Nam dextra ad invictum calibem semper erat in eo ferreis ambiebantur bratteolis. De ocreis quid dicam? Quae et cuncto exercitui solebant ferreae semper esse usui. In clipeo nihil apparuit nisi apparuit nisi ferrum. Caballus quoque illius animo et colore ferrum renitebat."
76. Cf. *Chalibinus*, meaning made of steel, *Ruodlieb*, fr. 1 v. 25, *fr.* 5 v. 80. As E. Vinaver, "King Arthur's Sword," *Bulletin of the John Rylands Library*, XL (1958), 516, points out, *calibs* is clearly Virgil's *chalybs*.

ample, suggests a religiously tinged political theory, i.e., the stone or, more exactly, the rock is the church which holds the sword, a symbol of secular rule, and will only permit the rightful king to wield it. By way of contrast, the sword in *Annwfu* is taken from the "otherworld," suggesting a religious connotation with non-Christian overtones. The most dominant theme associated with Arthur's sword, however, is the assurance of military and thus political superiority which it provides for its owner.

The sword as a symbol of rule and military prowess within a religious context can be traced to many corners of the world, including the central Asian steppes. Priscus, our best informant on the career of Attila, indicates that the Hunnic leader believed he would one day rule over Rome because God had revealed to him the sword of Mars which was held sacred by the rulers of the steppes. The sword was thought to be sacred because it was dedicated to the god of war. According to Priscus's story, the sword, after having been lost for many years, was rediscovered when an ox cut its foot on it while grazing in a field. Upon seeing the blood, the herder investigated, found the sword, and brought it to Attila, who is said to have believed that supremacy in war had been assured to him by possession of the sword of the god of war.[77]

It is not unlikely that Attila's appreciation of the sword as a symbol of power was derived from beliefs acquired by the Huns from their Alan subjects. It is known that the Alans worshipped as a god of war a naked sword fixed in the ground. This god of war was also seen by the Alans as the god of the "otherworld" who presided over the spirits of those ancestors who had died happy, i.e., in battle serving the god of war. These steppe asso-

77. Priscus, *frs.* 8, 10. See also Jordanes, *Getica*, ch. XXXV, who popularized Priscus's account for a Latin audience. The spread of motifs and stories from the steppes of central Asia to the north of Europe is amply demonstrated in, for example, *The Saga of King Heidrek the Wise*. In bk. 10 one finds the story of "The Battle of the Goths and the Huns." Curiously enough, a magic sword of sorts also plays a role in bk. 1 of this saga. The sword, Tyrfing, made its wielder invincible in battle. *Chalybs* (iron and thus sword) comes from the *Chalybes*, steppe iron workers from the Black Sea area (*Thesur. Ling. Lat. Onomasticon*, II, col. 369).

ciations of the political, military, and religious significance of the sword could only have been brought to Armorica by the Alans since they were the only steppe people to settle in that area.

The connection of steppe themes and the Arthurian legends may be brought into more than geographical proximity through the story of Conon Meriadoc, who plays an important role in some Arthurian materials. According to the preface of the *Life of Saint Geoznovoc,* an early eleventh-century document which includes information about Arthur, a certain Conon Meriadoc, who also plays a part in Geoffrey's *Historia,* landed in Armorica and killed the pagan warriors who opposed him; he kept their women alive, though, to use as wives and servants. He is said, however, to have had the women's tongues cut out so that they would not corrupt the Celtic language with their foreign speech. The theme of cutting out the tongues of women captives as developed in the preface to the *Life of Saint Geoznovoc* is unique in the Armorico-Welsh materials, and as far as I have been able to ascertain it does not appear in any other early medieval literature in Western Europe. Behind a unique theme may indeed lie a historical occurrence. It seems possible that in the late fifth century some of the Alans who had been settled in Armorica and who still spoke the old language, as suggested in the *Life of Saint Paul,* may not yet have been converted to Christianity but still worshipped the sword as a god of war who presided over the "otherworld" where the happy warriors found their ultimate home. On the other hand, it is also probable that Conon attacked Christian Alans, but that the story was changed over time in order to exonerate him from having committed such barbarisms against Christians. In any event, it is not impossible that a Celtic magnate—legend calls him Conon Meriadoc—intruded with his warband into an Alan area, killed the warriors who opposed him, and captured the women and cut out their tongues so that the strange barbarian speech from the steppes would not corrupt the purity of the conquerors' language.[78] Such

78. *Legenda sancti Geoznovii,* preface, 2 for Conon Meriadoc, and 3 for Arthur. Geoffrey, *Hist.,* chs. 81–88, 92, 115, 194. J. S. P. Tatlock, "The

Plate 1. Disc honoring the consulship of Aspar in 434.
(Source: R. Delbrueck, *Die Consular Diptychen und
verwandte Denkmäler*, pl. 35. Berlin and Leipzig, 1929.)

Plate 2. Alan and Vandal prisoners captured in 416.
(Source: R. Delbrueck, *Die Consular Diptychen und verwandte Dankmäler*, pl. 2. Berlin and Leipzig, 1929.)

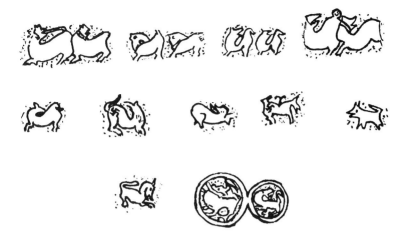

Plate 3. Four-footed animals in the Aquitanian style
showing central Asiatic influences.
(Source: Adapted from Nils Åberg, *The Occident and the
Orient in the Art of the Seventh Century*, p. 55, figs. 21, 1,
3, 4, 2, 10, 9, 8, 5, 7, 6. Stockholm, 1947.)

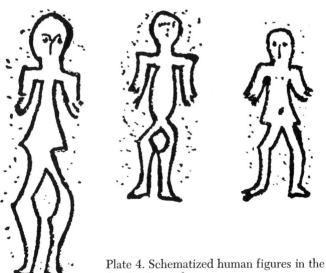

Plate 4. Schematized human figures in the
Aquitanian style.
(Source: Adapted from Nils Åberg, *The Occident
and the Orient in the Art of the Seventh
Century*, p. 57, figs. 23, 1, 2, 3. Stockholm, 1947.)

Plate 5a. Animal style ornamentation from Hungary.
(Source: Adapted from M. I. Rostovtzeff, "La centre de
l'Asie, la Russie, la Chine, et le style animal,"
Skythika, I [Prague, 1929], pl. 36.)

Plate 5b. Animal style ornamentation from Russia.
(Source: Adapted from V. A. Kusnetzov, "Alanskie Plemena
Severnogo Kaukaza," *Materialy i issledovaniia po
Arkheologii SSSR*, CVI [Moscow, 1962], pl. 11, fig. 2.)

Plate 6. Animal style ornamentation from Hungary.
(Source: Adapted from Joseph Hampel, *Alterthümer des
frühen Mittelalters in Ungarn*, pl. 97, fig. 2, pl. 162, fig. 3.
Brunswick, 1905.)

Plate 7a. Animal style ornamentation from Hungary.
(Source: Adapted from Joseph Hampel, *Alterthümer des
frühen Mittelalters in Ungarn*, fig. 1946. Brunswick, 1905.)

Plate 7b. Animal style ornamentation from Russia.
(Source: Adapted from Ernst Chantre, *Recherches
anthropologiques dans le Caucase*, III, pl. 8. Paris, 1885–1887.)

Plate 8. Illustrations of schematized
human figures from Russia.
(Source: Adapted from Ernst Chantre, *Recherches
anthropologiques dans le Caucase*, III, pl. 5, Paris, 1885–1887;
V. A. Kusnetzov, "Alanskie Plemena Severnogo Kaukaza,"
Materialy i issledovaniia po Arkheologii SSSR, CVI [Moscow,
1962], pl. 13, figs. 1, 2, 3; and from *The Art and
Architecture of Medieval Russia*, by Arthur Voyce, pl. 18.
Copyright 1967 by the University of Oklahoma Press.)

Plate 9a. Belt buckle with inscription in Aquitanian style.
(Source: L. Franchet, "Une colonie Scytho-Alaine
en Orléanais au Vᵉ siècle," *Revue scientifique*, LXVIII
[1930], 78, fig. 13a.)

Plate 9b. Rubbing of inscription on belt buckle.
(Source: L. Franchet, "Une colonie Scytho-Alaine
en Orléanais au Vᵉ siècle," *Revue scientifique*, LXVIII
[1930], 109, fig. 20.)

a story may also be a symbolic rendering of the Celts' attempts to destroy Alan culture. There are certainly no lack of examples in both fact and fiction for the brutal treatment of one ethnic group by another.

In the early Arthurian material there are two traditions concerning Arthur himself. In one, Arthur is the great Christian hero whom we see more fully developed in Geoffrey's *Historia*. In the other tradition, however, Arthur is something of an anti-hero; he is a rebellious king and a tyrant who, though apparently a Christian, is in conflict with the church and its holy men. In this second tradition Arthur is defeated in battle, he is unable to overcome a dragon, and he is humbled by saints on at least two separate occasions.[79]

In the *Life of Saint Carannog*, Arthur makes an altar into a table, but whatever is placed upon this new table is thrown off by a supernatural power. (Could Arthur's sacrilegious behavior in this pre-Geoffrey account presage the famous Round Table?) In the *Life of Saint Padarn*, Arthur attacks a holy man in an attempt to steal his cloak. The miraculous powers of the saint are such, however, that Arthur's greed and irreverence are thwarted when he is swallowed up by the earth and not freed until he begs the saint for forgiveness. Arthur, the "tyrant" in the *Life of Saint Padarn*, is portrayed in a similar manner in the *Life of Saint Cadoc*. In this account, Arthur is condemned for his lechery when he covets another man's woman, for his greed when he demands two-colored cattle as a wergild for his slain men, and for his irreverence when he threatens to violate the sanctuary of holy ground. From the *Life of Saint Gildas* by Caradoc we learn that Arthur was called *rex rebellus*, that he killed Gildas's brother, and that he was finally humbled by the saint: ". . . King Arthur, lamenting and crying, accepted the penance

Dates of the Arthurian Saints' Legends," *Speculum*, XIV (1939), 361–365, argues forcefully but unconvincingly that the internal date of 1019 is not accurate for the St. Geoznovoc preface and that the document is post-Geoffrey.

79. On these, see C. Grant Loomis, "King Arthur and the Saints," *Speculum*, VIII (1933), 478–482, and Tatlock, "Arthurian Saints' Legends," pp. 345–365.

imposed by the bishops who were there and emended his ways, as much as he could, until the end of his life."[80]

It has been argued that this image of Arthur is simply the theme of the "recalcitrant king" used by the writers of saints' lives to enhance the prestige of their subjects at the expense of an important lay figure. Moreover, this "bad image" of Arthur may well have represented the real life of the early medieval magnate better than the later heroic image did.[81] Marc Conomor, for example, seems to fit this prototype well, and we have much of our information about him from the *Life of Saint Samson* in which he is bested by the holy man.[82]

Rarely is it possible to learn how a particular legend evolved, and we would have to be very lucky indeed to ascertain who could have been the model for the "recalcitrant king" in the Arthur stories if it were not Arthur himself, who may not have existed as a historical individual at all but was instead developed in legend as representative of a particular type. Whatever or whoever Arthur might have been, it is desirable to consider the time in which he supposedly lived—in this case the latter part of the fifth century—if we are to learn anything about him.[83]

During the latter fifth century when Arthur is alleged to have flourished, one of the most popular holy men in Armorica and western Britain was Saint Germanus of Auxerre. This saint, who lived during the first half of the fifth century, made several trips to Britain where he gained great fame for his holiness and military abilities. In the latter capacity, he was called *dux belli* by both Bede, a usually reliable source, and Nennius. This, of course, has elicited notice because it is remarkably similar to Nennius's description of Arthur as *dux bellorum*. For both modern scholars and contemporaries, the major source of information concerning St. Germanus is his *Vita*, which was written during

80. *V. Carantoci*, chs. 3, 4, 5; *V. Paterni*, p. 188; *V. Cadoci*, pp. 24, 48–50, 54; *V. Gildae*, chs. 5, 7, 10.
81. Kenneth Jackson, "The Arthur of History," in *Arthurian Literature*, p. 2.
82. See the discussion by Chadwick, "Colonization," pp. 277–278.
83. On the development of legends and saints' legends in particular, see Hippolyte Delehaye, *The Legends of the Saints* (London, 1962).

the second half of the fifth century by Constantius, a contemporary of the real Arthur if he actually existed.[84]

In his career St. Germanus prevailed over many magnates,
and the theme of the "recalcitrant king" is well established in his
Vita. Among the magnates humbled by Germanus was the Alan
leader in Armorica, Eothar (Goar). Concerning a confrontation
between Germanus and Eothar, Constantius wrote,

Aetius . . . gave permission to Eothar, the savage king of the
Alans, to subdue Armorica; and Eothar, with the greed of a barbarian, was eager for the wealth of the area. So an old man [St.
Germanus] was pitted against an idolatrous king but, under
Christ's protection, the former proved greater and stronger than
all of his enemies. He set out quickly because preparations for
the campaign had already been made. The Alans were already
on the march and their armored horsemen crowded all the roads.
Nevertheless, our priest took the road moving toward the place
where he hoped to encounter the king who arrived after he did.
The march was already underway when the meeting took
place and thus the priest faced an armored magnate surrounded
by his followers. First the priest made requests through an interpreter. Then, as Eothar disregarded these requests, Germanus
scolded him. Finally, Germanus reached out his hand, grabbed
Eothar's horse's bridle, and stopped him, and with him he
stopped the entire army. At this the barbarian king's anger was
turned by God to admiration. Eothar was stunned by such firm-
ness, awed by such dignity, and moved by the strength of such
tenacious authority. The war gear and the commotion of arms
were set aside and their place was taken by the courtesies of
peaceful talks. Laying aside his arrogance, the king dismounted
and entered into a discussion which ended not in the satisfaction
of his desires but in satisfying the priest's requests.[85]

Every July 31, St. Germanus's day, this tableau, composed by
Constantius of Lyons about 480, was very probably presented
from the pulpits of churches throughout Armorica and Britain
during the early Middle Ages. How long would it have taken for
the deeds of the greedy and savage Eothar, who was the very

84. Levison, "Germanus von Auxerre," pp. 95–175, and cf. Jackson,
"Arthur of History," p. 9, for remarks on Bede and Nennius.
85. *V. Germani*, ch. 28.

115

model of a recalcitrant king, to become identified as Arthur in the popular mind? The merging of the deeds of Eothar with those of Arthur would seem to have been a very natural kind of confusion for the illiterate peoples of Britain and Armorica. Thus, it would seem that the popular identification of an Alan chief with the life of a hero saint may have helped to establish in the story of Arthur the legend that he was a kind of anti-hero.[86]

ALAN IMPACT ON THE WEST

When the Alans as nomads roamed the steppes of central Asia and south Russia, no able warrior was barred from playing a leadership role among his people. Military prowess and experience were the prerequisites for attaining such a position. After coming west, however, groups of Alans became imperial allies and changed their way of life as a result of having received land from Rome. The Alans in Gaul, for example, did not become *laeti*, who lived in semiautonomous communities and were responsible for producing the food and other necessities for their own sustenance. If the Alans had become *laeti*, substantial numbers of Alan fighting men would have had to have learned agricultural techniques and to have taken up farming as a full-time occupation. This would have meant that a large majority of Alan warriors would have been lost to imperial service, since the Alans' specialized kind of mounted warfare necessitated the practice of complicated tactical maneuvers such as the feigned retreat; they also needed the financial means to keep valuable mounts and other equipment. The Sarmatians who were settled by the empire as *laeti* and who fought in a manner similar to that of the Alans lost their effectiveness as did the Alans settled as *laeti* in Italy who had a lesser impact on history than their counterparts in Gaul.

Imperial officials in Gaul, wishing to preserve the military effectiveness of the Alans as cavalrymen, settled them on the basis of the hospitality system. According to this system, agree-

86. For a discussion of the various versions of Eothar's name including Euchar, Gochar, Gother, and Gobar, see ch. III, pp. 96–97.

ments were made between the Roman landholders of an area and the newcomers concerning the sharing of land, the economic dependents (slaves and *coloni*) dwelling thereon, and the income. Thus the Alans entered imperial society at the higher levels. As noted earlier, Roman landholders in the Orléanais resisted the division of land which was required by the hospitality agreements ordered by the imperial government; as a result, those hostile Gallo-Romans were driven out by their would-be partners. Therefore, in this area where Alan settlement seems to have been most influential, the newcomers did not share the wealth, but took it all and became the landed aristocracy.

During the second half of the fifth century, the Alan warriors who had thusly benefited by settlement within the empire were in a propitious position to become integrated into the class of *potentiores*, the powerful men who dominated local affairs. The Alans' frequently demonstrated propensity for assimilation enhanced their possibilities for integration. Early in the sixth century the city of Le Mans had a bishop named Alanus, and a generation later the first of a large number of Breton counts named Alan appeared in a family with distinguished Celtic connections.

The earlier discussions of Aspidius, the *senior loci* in the Orense, of Eutharic, the son-in-law of Theodoric the Ostrogoth, and of the several Goars who served as secular officials and gained prominence in the church under both Visigothic and Merovingian kings illustrate that men of Alan descent or those who obtained their names under the influence of people of Alan descent reached prominence in Western Europe during the early Middle Ages. Although the extent of Alan influence at this upper level of society cannot be ascertained because of the paucity of documents, we do learn of a very rich landholder of the Le Mans area named Alanus. He flourished early in the seventh century and gave his property to the Church of Le Mans after his son and heir was killed in a riding accident. In the southern part of the eastern area of Alan settlement near the town of Cheu (Yonne), one finds reference to a certain Asper, a landholder of note. At Courcy in Normandy a family which flourished during the early Middle Ages and traced its descent to the pre-Viking period bore the sobriquet *Alaniers*.[87]

The upper stratum of medieval society regarded hunting on horseback, the chase, as the premier outdoor sport. Hunting in such a manner was part of the Alans' way of life during their nomad days, and it seems probable that as landholders in early medieval Europe they continued to hunt the stag and the wolf, perhaps more for fun than was the case previously when hunting helped sustain their livelihood. In the hunt big, strong, and fast dogs were used to run the quarry to ground. One of the most renowned of these medieval hunting dogs was the now extinct Alan (med. Lat. *Alanus*) which, according to a modern authority on the history and origin of canine breeds, "derived originally from the Caucasus, whence it accompanied the fierce, fairhaired, and warlike Alani."[88]

Like the Alan horse in classical antiquity, the Alan dog in the Middle Ages gained great popularity. Later in the Middle Ages it was accorded the status of an heraldic symbol, and the town of Alano in Spain to this day bears two Alan dogs on its coat of arms. In the medieval sources, as well, there is some notice of those who bred the Alan dog. Many credited the Spanish with being the best producers of the breed, but others praised the breeders of Milan in Italy. It may be remembered that Milan is located in the midst of a number of Alan settlements which date back to the fifth century.[89]

87. *Actus pontificum Cenomannis*, ch. 11. On this text, see Walter Goffart, *The Le Mans Forgeries* (Cambridge, Mass., 1966), pp. 158, 226. Pardessus, II, 153: ". . . . in villas cognominatis Treviciaco, Melarione, Cadugio, Imantia, et Tornotrinse, de quibus Asper quondam ibidem tenuit . . ." Alexander Bergengruen, *Adel und Grundherrschaft in Merowingerreich* (Weisbaden, 1958), p. 219, mentions Asper as a Roman. Bergengruen tends to classify people as either Germans or Romans. It would have been more accurate, however, if he had used the classification German and non-German. For an incisive critique of Bergengruen's book, see the review by J. M. Wallace-Hadrill, *EHR*, LXXV (1960), 483–485. On the Alainiers of Courcy, see F. Galeron, *Statistique de l'arrondissement de Falaise*, II (Falaise, 1828), 393.

88. George R. Jesse, *Researches into the History of the British Dog*, II (London, 1886), 80–84, 116–118.

89. Jesse, *Researches*, II, 82, and appendix III, no. 22.

THE ASSIMILATION OF THE ALANS

By some criteria the history of the Alans in the West can be seen as a success story, while by other standards it may be considered a tale of disaster. According to the former, the Alans in Gaul and Italy were first integrated and then assimilated into early medieval culture. They left an enduring imprint on military tactics and upon the aristocracy. They influenced artistic motifs, the church, and literature. But the Alans founded no lasting state, and those in Africa and Constantinople disappeared without having a significant impact on posterity. In all but the most scholarly circles the Alan people in the West have vanished as thoroughly as the *canis Alani*, their famed hunting dog of the Middle Ages. The Alans' propensity for assimilation, which often helped them to survive and flourish, was instrumental and probably decisive in bringing about their ultimate disappearance. But even today in modern France there survives a little understood epithet which reminds us of the role the Alans played in the conflicts of the early Middle Ages. The saying is not complimentary, however, and illustrates an anti-Alan prejudice which survives in what today is Normandy: "cet homme est violent et allain."[90]

90. *La Grande Encyclopédie* (Paris, 1886), I, 1118.

Appendixes

Tacitus
Ignores the Alans

S OME historians have argued that Nero, during the last year or so of his life, planned a campaign against the Alans with the object of taking control of the pass at Dariel (Caucasian Gates).[1] Knowledge of this alleged campaign is based primarily upon a remark by Tacitus (*Hist.*, I, 6): ". . . multi ad hoc numeri e Germania ac Britannia et Illyrico, quos idem Nero electos praemissosque ad claustra Caspiarum et bellum, quod in Albanos parabat, opprimendis Vindicis coeptis revocaverat. . . ." Additional support is given by Suetonius (*Nero*, 19): "parabat et ad Caspias portas expeditionem conscripta ex Italicis senum pedum tironibus nona legione, quam Magni Alexandri phalanga appellabat."

Tacitus clearly says that the campaign was to be against the Albani and that the purpose of the effort was to gain command of the Caspian Gates. Scholars have shown, however, that Roman notions of the geography of this area were not always accurate. According to some, Tacitus may well have meant the Caucasian Gates rather than the Caspian Gates, and, if this were the case, then Nero's campaign was directed not against the Albani but against the Alans. It is possible that Tacitus was thusly mistaken,

1. Mommsen, *Röm. Gesch.*, V, 393–394; A. Anderson, "Alexander and the Caspian Gates," *Transactions of the American Philosophical Association*, LIX (1928), 144–147; Ronald Syme, "Flavian Wars and Frontiers," *CAH*, XI (1936), 143; and Sanford, "Nero and the East," p. 95. Cf. Debevoise, *Parthia*, p. 197.

and that Suetonius was also in error. Other Greek and Roman writers of the time often confused the two passes.[2] Moreover, Tacitus seems to have had a penchant for either confusing the Alani with the Albani or for ignoring the Alani altogether.[3] Though there is certainly room to doubt Tacitus's accuracy in recording Nero's campaign, an entirely new reading, i.e., *Alani* for Albani and Caucasian Gates for Caspian Gates, is, at least, equally dubious. The Alans were a primitive nomadic people scattered in small bands throughout the steppes, and the idea of Roman legions pursuing these fast horsemen over thousands of miles of steppe is absurd.[4] In addition, the Alans had supported Roman policy against Parthia in A.D. 35 and were still supporting a Roman anti-Parthian policy in A.D. 72 after Nero's death. The

2. Anderson, "Alexander and the Caspian Gates," pp. 130–163; *Alexander's Gate: Gog Magog and the Enclosed Nations* (Cambridge, Mass., 1932), pp. 15–16; and Sanford, "Nero and the East," p. 94. Täubler, "Alanen," p. 19.

3. Tacitus, *Ann.*, II, 68, tells of a certain Verones who "effugere ad Armenios, inde albanos Heniochosque et consanguineum sibi regem Scytharum conatus est." In this passage, Tacitus seems to have been influenced by Valerius Flaccus, *Argonautica*, VI 42ff: "Miserat ardentes, mox ipse secutus, Alanos Heniochosque truces iam pridem infensus Anausis, pacta quod Albano coniux Medea tyranno." But where Valerius has *Alani* Tacitus has *Albani*. Cf. Täubler, "Alanen," p. 14, n. 3.

From Orosius (*Hist.*, VII, 34, 5) has been gleaned what some have considered a fragment (7) of Tacitus's *Histories*: "Theodosius . . . maximas illas Scythicas gentis formidatasque cunctis mairobus, Alexandro quoque illi Magno, sicut Pompeius Corneliusque testati sunt, evitatis, . . . hoc est Alanos Hunos et Gothos, incunctanter adgressus magnis multisque proeliis vicit." Since the Huns were unknown in the West until the fourth century, this remark apparently attributed to Tacitus by Orosius could not have been written by the former. In addition, the combination "Alans, Huns, and Goths" is peculiar to the later Roman empire. See Täubler, "Alanen," p. 14, n. 3, and Thompson, *Attila and the Huns*, pp. 15ff.

Tacitus, *Ann.*, VI, 33, discusses an invasion of Parthia in A.D. 72–74 in the following manner: ". . . contra Pharasmanes adiungere Albanos, accire Sarmatas, quorum sceptuchi utrimque donis acceptis more gentico diversa induere. Sed Hiberi locorum potentes Caspia via Sarmatam in Armenios raptim effundunt." Whereas Tacitus refers to the invaders as Sarmatians and mentions their "wand carriers," Josephus, *De Bell. Jud.*, VII, 4, 244ff, whose information on Parthian affairs is more reliable than that of Tacitus, calls the invaders Alans. See E. Täubler, *Die Parthernachrichten bei Josephus* (Berlin, 1904), pp. 30–33, 54, 58–59, and Debevoise, *Parthia*, p. xxix. For differences between the Sarmatians and the Alans, see M. I. Rostovtzeff, "Sarmatae and Parthians," p. 92.

4. See ch. I, pp. 23–24.

Alans should be viewed as enemies of the Parthians, and they were probably seen in that light by Rome. Whether or not there was a truce, Parthia was Rome's great enemy in the East. An enemy of Parthia would generally be rewarded by Rome rather than attacked.[5]

Nero, who seems to have regarded himself as another Alexander the Great and apparently dreamed of conquests in the east, could fulfill that self-image by conquering the Parthians as Alexander had conquered the Persians.[6] It seems very possible that Nero would have planned a massive campaign into the heart of Parthian territory despite the existence of a truce (plans for war are usually made in times of peace) in an effort to subject the Albani and seize control of the Caspian Gates.

5. Debevoise, *Parthia,* pp. 179–202.
6. Sanford, "Nero and the East," pp. 86–88, makes a strong case for the influence of the Alexander image on Nero but concludes that Nero then sought to campaign against the Alans rather than against the Parthians.

Arrian
against the Alans

As observed in the preface, the nominalist approach used in this study must be qualified in certain circumstances. In part this appendix provides an example of the modification of the nominalist approach and at the same time illustrates the quality of the evidence that is necessary to support such modification.

Arrian, the legate of Cappadocia under the Emperor Hadrian, is known from several ancient sources to have conducted a military campaign against the *Alani* in A.D. 134. He was also considered to be a historian of importance. Among his historical works was the *Alanica* or *History of the Alans*. Only a small part of this work, *Acies contra Alanos*, has survived.[1] This fragment can be divided into two distinct though not unrelated parts. The first appears to be a copy, perhaps somewhat edited, of the marching orders which Arrian issued for his campaign against the Alans who had invaded Cappadocia. The second section, an outline of the tactics to be used against these enemies, gives some information on Alan tactics as well. Arrian, whose literary talents and aspirations are well known to modern scholars, refers to the Alans in the only surviving fragment of the *Alanica* as Scythians.

1. J. Sheffer in 1664 produced the earliest edition of *Acies contra Alanos*. The most recent edition is that of A. G. Roos (1928), which has been slightly modified by G. Wirth (1968).

There seems to be no doubt, however, that Arrian has merely shown a preference for the more literary term *Scythians* in this particular section of the *Alanica,* but that he was in fact talking about the Alans.[2]

The second purpose of this appendix is to provide for the first time in English an interpretative translation of *Contra Alanos.* This document illustrates not only the detail and care with which Arrian prepared the marching orders for this campaign, but also the significance of his forthcoming confrontation with the Alans. The very size of the Roman forces suggests the importance attached to repulsing the invasion of the Alans. The text, taken as a whole, exemplifies the Romans' high regard for Alan military prowess as well as the seriousness to the empire of the Alan thrust into Cappadocia.

TACTICS AGAINST THE ALANS

The entire army will form only one column. At the head of this column will ride the cavalry in pairs of two and detailed to reconnoiter. After them will come some light infantry, javelin men and slingers, divided into two groups under the command of decurions. These will be followed by the regiment of Isaurian cavalry, which will have been joined by four cohorts of Rhaetians and a unit of Kolones under the command of Daphnus the Corinthian. Marching behind these forces will be first the Iturians and then the Cyreneans. All these troops will be commanded by Demetrius. The Celtic cavalry, formed into units and riding two by two, will follow Demetrius's men. They will be led by the same officer who commanded them in camp.

Proceeding the Celtic cavalry will be the infantry, composed equally of Italians and Cyreneans, with their standards going in front of them. Pulcher, the leader of the Italians, will command the lot. The Bosphorian infantry commanded by Lamprocles will march behind these forces, and following them will be the nomads

2. E. Schwartz, "Arrianus," *RE,* II, cols. 1230–1247; Dain, "Les stratégistes Byzantins," pp. 331–332; and P. Stadter, "Flavius Arrianus: The New Xenophon," *Greek, Roman, and Byzantine Studies,* VIII (1967), 155–161.

under the command of Verus. These four units of infantry will be preceded by a troop of archers. A squadron of Archaean cavalry will patrol both flanks of the infantry to provide added protection. After these infantry units will ride the elite cavalry followed by the legionary cavalry and then the full complement of catapults. Following them will be the insignia of the Fifteenth Legion and its commander Valens along with the legate, the chiliarchs, and the centurions of the first cohort. Close by the insignia some light infantry will march. Behind it will be the legionary infantry in ranks of four. After the Fifteenth Legion will come the insignia of the Twelfth Legion around which will form up the chiliarchs and the centurions. The Twelfth will march in the same manner as the Fifteenth.

These heavily armed troops will be backed up by the allies from lesser Armenia, heavily armed Trapezuntians, the Colchians, and the Rhizian lancers. Following them will be the Aplanian infantry. Secundus, the leader of the Aplanians, will command this whole force of allies. The baggage will follow immediately behind these units. A troop of Gothic cavalry under its commander will bring up the rear of the entire line of march.

The infantry officers will march with their companies to the right and to the left of the line of march. Two units of cavalry, the Galacians and the Italians, will skirt the infantry's line of march. The cavalry will form only one file along each of the two flanks.

Xenophon,[3] the general-in-chief, will have no fixed position; he will post himself wheresoever it is necessary to maintain order. From time to time he will place himself in front of the legionary eagles and sometimes at the head of the entire line of march. He will correct those who neglect their formation and will praise those who conserve it. Thus the army will advance in its appointed manner.

When the army comes to the place where battle is to be given, all the cavalry will detach itself from the line of march and take up positions in front and on the flanks. It will deploy in squares

3. Stadter, "Arrianus," pp. 155–161, has established that Arrian's full name was Flavius Arrianus Xenophon.

at different locations. The cavalry detailed for reconnoitering will take an advanced position so that it may observe the enemy. A signal will be given, at which the soldiers will form themselves up and make ready their weapons. Care will be taken that this be done in silence; the soldiers once armed and ready will be in position to fight. The infantry will be deployed in a horned formation with its wings resting on rises to the right and to the left. On the right flank will be the Armenians under Vusaces and Arbelus. They will hold the highest ground because they are all bowmen. The cohort of Italian infantry and those others commanded by Pulcher, the leader of the Italians, will deploy on the slope below the archers. Pulcher will have under him the commanders of the Armenians, Vusaces and Arbelus, and the cavalry which they lead.

The other wing, which includes the allied infantry, the Trapezuntians, and the Rhizian lancers, will be formed and emplaced on the heights to the left. They will have in front of them two hundred Aplanians and one hundred Cyreneans so that these heavy infantry can protect the archers while they fire their arrows down on the enemy. The Fifteenth Legion, which is the stronger of the two legions, will be based on the rise to the right, and its infantry will extend itself from there toward the center. The infantry of the Twelfth Legion will fill the empty space up to the rise on the left; it will extend itself as far as it can to the slope of the hill. The legionaries will be formed in ranks of eight deep and in close order; those who have spears will be placed in the first four ranks and those with pikes in the four ranks behind them. The men of the first line will present their spears at the approach of the enemy; care will be taken to warn the troops to hold the iron point at the height of the oncoming horses' chests. Those of the second, of the third, and of the fourth lines will be in position to throw their spears. They will be directed, accordingly, to aim their strikes accurately at the right time in order to knock down the horses and throw the riders. The impact of the spear with its flexible iron point and the weight of each rider's shield and armor will make it impossible for him to remount and use his horse again. A ninth rank, composed of archers, will be positioned behind the eighth; this rank will include nomads, Cyreneans, Bosphorians, and Iturians. The positions for the catapults will be marked out on the two hills behind the entire army; they will be fired on the enemy from a distance.

All the cavalry grouped in squadrons and in eight units of one hundred men each are to deploy while supporting the infantry. These horsemen will spread out from flank to flank with the heavy infantry positioned in front of them. Two units of one hundred men each will be posted behind the archers on the flanks; six of the hundred-man units will deploy behind the legionary infantry. All the mounted archers will be placed very near the infantry phalanx so as to be in position to fire over their heads. All who are armed with spears, lances, swords, or axes will deploy on the flanks facing away from the center and will await a signal to go into action. A detail will be designated as an escort for Xenophon; this will be formed of elite cavalry units, two hundred legionary infantry, Xenophon's regular bodyguards, centurions, the prefect's bodyguards, and selected cavalry officers. One hundred light lancers will stand by to deliver orders to various parts of the formation during the battle. This entire force will act as a reserve to be used wherever it might be needed. Valens, the commander of the Fifteenth Legion, will lead the right and all the cavalry; the left will be under the command of the chiliarchs of the Twelfth Legion.

When everything is being set in order, the troops will remain silent. When the enemy comes into range of our missiles and the attack begins, everyone will set up a very loud and terrible war cry. At the same time the catapults will hurl heavy missiles and stones. The archers and all the troops who have weapons to hurl will shower the enemy with their arrows, spears, and javelins. With missiles showered on the enemy even by the allies, it is unlikely that the enemy will be successful. It is hoped that this vast mass of missiles will cause the confusion and the ruin of men and horses, and that the enemy will lose the desire and the

ARRIAN AGAINST THE ALANS

strength to push home its attack. If, however, they do attack the
heavy infantry, it is necessary, as soon as possible, to move up
the second and the third ranks and have them press closely together shoulder to shoulder and shield to shield so that they will
be firmly braced for the very violent shock of the enemy cavalry
attack. The fourth rank will hurl its spears over the heads of the
soldiers in front of them in an indiscriminate manner at either
the riders or the horses. When the enemy has been hurled back
and takes flight, the infantry will open its ranks and half of the
cavalry, but not the troops of the hundred-man units, will charge
after them. These units will pursue the enemy in a vigorous manner, whereas the other half of the cavalry will follow them more
slowly, keeping its formation strictly in order so as to be in position to support the former if the Scythians make an abrupt turn
and to replace the first unit should it become tired. At the same
time as the cavalry advances, the Armenian archers and the remaining troops who use missile weapons will move out of their
positions and will try to be in position to support the cavalry by
deploying in range to fire their missiles at the enemy. Thus the
enemy will be given no respite. All the legionary infantry will
move out to the front, and marching no more quickly than they
do ordinarily, they will follow the light troops. Thus if, contrary
to our hopes, the Scythian cavalry regains momentum and re-
establishes its attack to the point of forcing our troops to retreat,
the legionary infantry will serve to support them and to give
them the means of reforming themselves.

This will all be executed in case of a precipitous flight on the
part of the enemy. But, if instead of giving ground against the
legions the Scythian cavalry retires to the rear after having sus-
tained the hail of missiles and seems to prepare to turn the
flanks so as to fall on the back of the army, I do not want the
light troops to make even the slightest move to spread out on
the wings. It has been learned by experience that this maneuver
only exposes the infantry which will then be scattered easily and
quickly destroyed. The entire defense in this situation will come
from the cavalry which will repulse the enemy. For this purpose,

it is necessary to deploy it to the wings menaced by the Scythians and to signal to the cavalry units at the rear of the legions to join themselves to the groups which have from the outset been positioned behind the wings. Together these cavalry units will form a hook-shaped line. When the Scythians are compelled to expose themselves in turning the wings, the cavalry is to attack them quickly. The cavalry is to charge with swords and axes and it is to fire without delay. For since both the Scythians and their horses are without heavy armor . . . (The manuscript breaks off here.)

Alan Place Names

I N RECENT years the use of toponymical evidence and the methods for evaluating these data have been the subject of considerable discussion and criticism.[1] Since such evidence is frequently used in this work, some comment on the procedures that were followed and the assumptions that were made seems to be in order.

The methods for establishing that a particular place name or group of place names represents Alan settlement or influence obviously vary according to the evidence which the vagaries of time have permitted to survive. For example, the *Chronica Gallica* provides reliable evidence for the establishment of an Alan settlement in the Orléanais by the order of the Roman military commander in Gaul in 442. This chronicle further indicates that many of the important landowners in the area resisted the settlement and were driven out. Other sources contend that the Alans and their descendants functioned in an active military capacity in the Orléanais and further to the west for decades after the settlements were established. Further evidence maintains that their descendants influenced various aspects of life

1. See, for example, Hans Walther, "Namenkunde und Archäologie im Dienste frühgeschichtlicher Forschung," *Probleme des frühen Mittelalters in archäologischer und historischer Sicht* (Berlin, 1966), pp. 155–168; Wallace-Hadrill's review of Bergengruen in *EHR*; and F. T. Wainwright, *Archaeology and Place-Names and History* (London, 1962).

through the early Middle Ages and later. Surviving medieval documents provide us with information concerning a number of place names in the Orléanais which embody some element of the word *Alani*. These documents, however, date from no earlier than the eleventh century. Thus, there is a time gap of some six centuries between Alan settlement in the Orléanais and the earliest surviving written evidence for place names which might be illustrative of that settlement.

A time gap of such magnitude must raise doubts concerning the direct relation between the original Alan settlement and these place names. Such doubts are given substance, for example, by the place name Domnus Alanus (modern Domalain, Ille-et-Vilaine), which has the same meaning as Sanctus Alanus. Such a place name could not be illustrative of the original Alan settlement since the Alans were pagans in the 440s, and it is unlikely that a St. Alan existed at that time. In addition, the use of *domnus*, a reduced form of *dominus*, gained currency in Gaul about 700, or almost 250 years after the original Alan settlement in the Orléanais. It should be noted, however, that a St. Alan did flourish in northwestern Gaul in approximately 700. Yet the earliest surviving document which provides a reference of the town of Domalain dates from about 1330, some 600 years after the saint had achieved his greatest popularity. Domalain was a small, unimportant place during the Middle Ages, and there was little or no reason for it to be mentioned in the relatively few documents which the primitive life of the age permitted.

The time span between Domalain's first mention in the sources and the life of St. Alan is similar to the period which elapsed between the Alan settlement in the Orléanais and the earliest mentions of place names in that area which had an Alan- element. Similarly, as well, the places with names that seem to owe their origin to some kind of Alan influence were also insignificant during the Middle Ages. That Alan names should be attached to unimportant places is consistent with the nature of Alan settlement within the framework of the Roman hospitality system by which the newcomers were given a share of an agrarian estate; elements of erstwhile manors appear frequently with names illustrative of Alan influence. Thus, the villa or court which came under the control of an Alan magnate might well have come to be called Allainville or Alaincourt. In short, we know that there were Alan settlements in the Orléanais, that the Alans influenced various aspects of life throughout northwestern Gaul during the early and high Middle Ages, and that a noteworthy number of place names in this area were influenced by the Alans (see below). It cannot be proven that some of the places with modern names like Allainville and Alaincourt were the original sites of Alan settlements, but such an hypothesis is not unreasonable.

An essential element in accepting the Alan origin of the names listed below is reasonable confidence in the meaning of the Alan-element found therein. The word *Alani* (Gr. 'Aλavoί) does not appear in the Western sources before the first century A.D., and Alans themselves did not settle in the West before the fifth century. No place names in Western Europe that bear an Alan-element can be shown to date from before the fifth century. Thus, it is justifiable to follow the general scholarly consensus which identifies such place names as having some relation to the *Alani*. Parenthetically, it may be noted that no other explanation for the place name element Alan- has been advanced which has found even minimal acceptance.[2]

The changes in pronunciation and orthography from the Middle Ages to the present have done much to make various forms of names difficult to recognize. The modern French Allaines, for example, had as its medieval form Alania, suggesting an area of

2. To the works cited in ch. III, n. 78, add Dante Olivieri, *Dizionario di Toponomastica Lombarda*, 2nd ed. (Milan, 1961), p. 17, and Galeron, *Statistique de Falaise*, II, 393. Some of the curious remarks of W. E. D. Allen, *David Allens: The History of a Family Firm, 1857–1957* (London, 1957), pp. 7–8, 23–25, and a letter quoted by Vernadsky, *Origins of Russia*, pp. 52–53, are worth noting: "The common personal name Alan [Alain, Alaunus] is of Breton origin. . . . There were settlements of Alans in Armorica in the fifth century A.D. . . . The name Alanus 'the Alan' must have been common from that time." Thus having a Breton origin does not necessarily mean having a Celtic origin. See Wagner, *Getica*, pp. 11–12, on Alan as a personal name.

Alan settlement; but in parts of southern France and northern Italy Alagna also developed from Alania. The dropping of the initial "A" from Alan- constituted a change from the medieval Alan d'Riano to the modern Landriano or an equally understandable change from Molendinum de Alanha to the modern Moulin de Lagne. Because of orthographic difficulties, some scholars have hesitated to classify elements such as Alen- and Allen- as being derived from Alan-. In 857, however, we have a reference to Alancianus, which in 1157 was called Alencianus. A nearby swamp which took its name from the town was called in a document of 1317 stagnum de Alensan. Conversely, Courtalain was Curia Alemi in 1095 but Curia Alani in 1128. The earliest reference to the modern Alenson is the thirteenth-century Alansonum.

There are even stranger changes: the Ecclesia de Alanis, which first appears in documents of the tenth century, is today Alos. The earliest extant mention of the town Allan (Drôme) comes from a document of the twelfth century and appears as Alondo. Forms such as Allonne and Allone to which Alondo seems very similar are Celtic and derive from Alauna and its variants. Yet, in the immediate area of Allan, a band of Alans are known to have been settled by imperial order about A.D. 440. In addition, these Alans were settled on deserted lands making it more than likely that they would give their name to at least a few places in the area. Nearby Allan is the town of Alansonum, mentioned above, which flourished during the Middle Ages. There is also the case of Ailan- as representative of Alan-. The town of Aillianville was Allanville in the seventeenth century and Allenville in the twelfth century. By way of contrast Alaincourt-aux-Boeufs was Alanum in 836, Alamnum in 936, and Ailain in 1305. Perhaps the most bizarre rendering of the *Alani* is their appearance in a medieval manuscript as the *Ellaini*.[3]

In medieval documents we see great orthographic variation, and we know that scribes cared little for precise spelling; that a name could be recognized was sufficient. In short, when using place names the evidence of a historical and archaeological na-

3. For Ellaini, see *Chronographus anni CCCLIII*, ch. 105, 101.

ture which can be associated with them seems to be of more importance than the earliest surviving mention of the name in a document or the "pure" spelling of the name.

By way of impressing upon the reader an element of balance, it should be noted that the several dozen place names listed below, which are suggested to be of Alan origin or representative of Alan influence, are a very small fraction of the tens of thousands of place names in modern France, Switzerland, Italy, and Spain which have been examined. These relatively few Alan place names have been garnered from an extensive study of toponymical dictionaries and published medieval documents. The preoccupation here with Alan place names should not mislead the reader into viewing them as disproportionately numerous in comparison with the total number of place names in the areas under discussion.

The arguments from the literary and archaeological evidence which support the interpretation of the place names listed below are to be found where the names are integrated into the narrative. Appropriate references to documents and scholarly works are listed in this appendix with each entry. The entries are in alphabetical order.

LIST

1. Aillianville (Haute-Marne): Allenville, ca. 1172; Alainville, 1402; Ailainville, 1446; Allanville, 1628. A. Roserot, *Dictionnaire topographique du département de la Haute-Marne* (Paris, 1903), p. 2.

2. Alagna (Com. Piemonte). D. Olivieri, *Dizionario di Toponomastica Lombarda*, p. 50, and *Dizionario Enciclopedico dei comuni d'Italia* (= *D.E.*) (Rome, 1950), II, 61. G. Giordani, *La colonia tedesca di Alagna-Valsesia e il suo dialetto* (Torino, 1881), p. 117, points out that German domination of Alagna is a product of the high Middle Ages.

3. Alagna (St. Germano). *D.E.*, I.1, 727.

4. Alagna Lomellina (Pavia). *D.E.*, I.2, 365.

5. Alaigne (Aude): Alaniano, 1129; Castrum de Alagnano, 1252; Alahan, 1257. A. Longnon, *Le noms de lieux de la France* (Paris, 1920), no. 534; A. Dauzat and C. Rostaing, *DNL*, p. 8; H. Gröhler, *Ueber Ursprung und Bedeutung der französischen Ortsnamen* (Heidelberg, 1913–1935), II, 7; and A. Sabarthès, *Dictionnaire topographique du département de l'Aude* (Paris, 1912), p. 5.

137

6. Alain (Ain). Dauzat and Rostaing, *DNL*, p. 8, and Edouard Philipon, *Dictionnaire topographique du département de l'Ain* (Paris, 1911), p. 5.

7. Alain (Loire-Inférieure). H. Quilgars, *Dictionnaire topographique du département de la Loire-Inférieure* (Nantes, 1906), p. 2.

8. Alain, also called Alaincourt-aux-Boeufs (Meurthe-et-Moselle): Alanum, 836; Alamnum, 936; Alannum, 965; Ailain and Allein, 1305. Cf. Dauzet and Rostaing, *DNL*, p. 10, and see Henri Lepage, *Dictionnaire topographique du département de la Meurthe* (Paris, 1862), p. 3.

9. Alaincourt (Aisne): Halincurt, 1168; Elleincourt, 1174; Allaincourt, 1189. Dauzat and Rostaing, *DNL*, p. 8, and Auguste Matton, *Dictionnaire topographique du département de l'Aisne* (Paris, 1871), p. 4.

10. Alaincourt (Ardennes): Alaincort, 1229. Dauzat and Rostaing, *DNL*, p. 8.

11. Alaincourt (Eure): Alaincuria and Alanicuria, both 1242; Ailancourt, 1303. Dauzat and Rostaing, *DNL*, p. 8; Gröhler, *Ursprung*, II, 295; and B. E. de Blosseville, *Dictionnaire topographique du département de l'Eure* (Paris, 1877), p. 3.

12. Alaincourt (Haute-Saône). Dauzat and Rostaing, *DNL*, p. 8.

13. Alaincourt, also called Alaincourt-la-Côte (Meurthe-et-Moselle): Allaincourt, 1549. Dauzat and Rostaing, *DNL*, p. 8; Gröhler, *Ursprung*, II, 295; and Lepage, *La Meurthe*, p. 2.

14. Alains (Eure): Fief aux Alains, 1394. de Blosseville, *L'Eure*, p. 3.

15. Alainville, also Allainville aux Bois (Seine-et-Oise): villa Alleni, ninth century. Dauzat and Rostaing, *DNL*, p. 8, and Hippolyte Cocheris, *Dictionnaire des anciens noms des communes du département de Seine-et-Oise* (Versailles, 1874), p. 27.

16. Alan (Haute-Garonne). Dauzat and Rostaing, *DNL*, p. 8.

17. Alancianus (Aude), no longer exists: Alancianus, 857; Alencianus, 1157; Alaussanum, 1360; nearby stagnum de Alaussano, stagnum de Alausa, stagnum de Alensan, 1317–1639. Sabarthès, *L'Aude*, p. 5.

18. Alançon (Drôme). J. Brun-Durand, *Dictionnaire topographique du département de la Drôme* (Paris, 1891), p. 3.

19. Alange (Badajoz), also Alanje. *Enciclopedia Universal ilustrada* (Barcelona, 1907–19– –), IV, 22.

20. Alaniers (Ain): Alagnier, eighteenth century. Philipon, *L'Ain*, p. 5.

21. Alanis (Seville). *Enciclopedia Universal ilustrada*, IV, 22.

22. Alano (Huesca). *Enciclopedia Universal ilustrada*, IV, 22.

23. Alano di Piave (San Antonio). *D.E.*, I.1, 916.

24. Aleins (Ain): Alens, 1325; Aleins, eighteenth century. Philipon, *L'Ain*, p. 5.

25. Alençon (Drôme): Alansonum, 1298; Alansone, 1355; Capella de Alensone, 1499; Alansone, 1509. Brun-Durand, *La Drôme*, p. 4.

ALAN PLACE NAMES

26. Alenya (Pyrénées-Orientales): Allenius. Dauzat and Rostaing, *DNL*, p. 10.

27. Algans (Tarn). *La Grande Encyclopédie* (Paris, 1887), II, 147; cf. E. Nègre, *Les noms de lieux du Tarn*, 2nd ed. (Paris, 1957), p. 43.

28. Allaigne (Ain). Philipon, *L'Ain*, p. 5.

29. Allain (Calvados). C. Hippeau, *Dictionnaire topographique du département du Calvados* (Paris, 1883), p. 3.

30. Allain (Morbihan). M. Rosenzweig, *Dictionnaire topographique du département du Morbihan* (Paris, 1870), p. 2.

31. Allain (Torino): Allein; Allianum; Allain. *D.E.*, I.1, 70; I.2, 40.

32. Allaines (Eure-et-Loir): Alena, 1130; Allene, 1165. Longnon, *Noms de lieux*, no. 534; Dauzat and Rostaing, *DNL*, p. 10; and Lucien Merlet, *Dictionnaire topographique du département d'Eure-et-Loir* (Paris, 1861), p. 2.

33. Allains (Somme): Alania, 1095. Longnon, *Noms de lieux*, no. 534, and Dauzat and Rostaing, *DNL*, p. 8.

34. Allains, les (Eure). de Blosseville, *L'Eure*, p. 3.

35. Allainville, also Allainville-en-Beuce (Loiret): Aleinvilla, 1236. Dauzat and Rostaing, *DNL*, p. 8, and Gröhler, *Ursprung*, II, 295.

36. Allainville-en-Drouais (Eure-et-Loir): Alainville, ca. 1100; Alanvilla, ca. 1160. Dauzat and Rostaing, *DNL*, p. 8; Gröhler, *Ursprung*, II, 295; and Merlet, *Eure-et-Loir*, p. 2.

37. Allamont (Meurthe-et-Moselle): possibly Elemcurt, 893; Alani monti, 1194; Allamon, fifteenth century. Dauzat and Rostaing, *DNL*, p. 8.

38. Allan (Drôme): Alon, 1138; castrum de Alondo, 1345; Santa Maria de Alondo, 1183; Alan, eighteenth century. Dauzat and Rostaing, *DNL*, p. 8, and Brun-Durand, *La Drôme*, p. 5.

39. Allancourt (Marne): Halancourt, 1735. A. Longnon, *Dictionnaire topographique du département de la Marne* (Paris, 1891), p. 2.

40. Alland'huy (Ardennes). *La Grande Encyclopédie*, II, 250.

41. Allegno, Villa d', also Villa Dallegno (Verona). Olivieri, *Lombarda*, p. 53.

42. Allens, also Alens. Arthur Jacot, *Schweizerisches Ortslexikon* (Lucerne, 1969), p. 5.

43. Alos (Tarn): Alanus, Alas, twelfth and thirteenth centuries. Edmond Cabié, *Droits et possessions du comte de Toulouse dans l'Albigeois au milieu du XIIIᵉ siècle* (Albi, 1900), pp. 51, 52, 61, 96, 104, 167; Cabié, "Alos en Albigeois aux Xᵉ et XIᵉ siècles," pp. 122–129; Louis de Lacger, *États administratifs des anciens diocèses d'Albi, de Castres, et de Lavaur* (Albi, 1929), pp. 86, 92, 146, 149, 208, 278, 279, 337, 339, 340, 342, 344; and Nègre, *Tarn*, pp. 34–35.

44. Bodieuc, formerly Alanczon (Morbihan), 1199. Rosenzweig, *Morbihan*, pp. 16, 297.

45. Brèche d'Allanz (Hautes-Pyrénées). Karl Baedeker, *Southern France*, 6th ed. (Leipzig, 1914), p. 154.

46. Courtalain (Eure-et-Loir): Curia Alemi, 1095; Cortollein, 1120; Curia Alani, 1128; Curtoslenum, 1130; Curtoslain, 1132. Merlet, *Eure-et-Loir*, p. 55.

47. Domalain (Ille-et-Vilaine): Domnus Alanus, ca. 1330. Longnon, *Noms de lieux*, nos. 1525, 1575, and Dauzat and Rostaing, *DNL*, p. 325.

48. Goarec, also Gouarec (Côtes-du-Nord). Dauzat and Rostaing, *DNL*, p. 325.

49. La London (Ain): Aqua de Alandons, 1397. Philipon, *L'Ain*, p. 230.

50. Landriano (Pavia): Alan d'Riano, twelfth century. *D.E.*, I.1, 747.

51. Lanet (Aude): Villa de Alianto and Alane, both in 951; Alane-tum, 1320; Alhanetum, 1331; Ailhanet, 1409. Sabarthès, *L'Aude*, pp. 195–196, and Bachrach, "Another Look at the Barbarian Settlement in Southern Gaul," p. 356, n. 9.

52. Langais (Indre-et-Loire): Alangaviense vici and Alingaviensi, late sixth century. Gregory, *Hist.*, X, 31; *G.M.*, ch. 15, pp. 485, 498. A question is raised regarding whether this name derives from a hypothetical Germanic name "Allin" or the well-documented Indo-Iranian name Alan. On this problem, see Longnon, *Géographie*, pp. 260–262, and Morlet, *Toponymie*, p. 51. In *Hist.*, X, 31, Gregory associates Saint Martin with the village of Langais, indicating that he built a church there. Among Gregory's contemporaries there were efforts to associate Saint Martin with the conversion of the Alans. On this, see Bachrach, "Alans in Gaul," pp. 486–487. Cf. J-X. Carré de Busserolle, *Dictionnaire géographique, historique, et biographique d'Indre-et-Loire* (Tours, 1882), IV, 15.

53. Lansac (Pyrénées-Orientales). Dauzat and Rostaing, *DNL*, p. 365.

54. Moulin de Lange (Aude): Molendinum de Alanha, 1279. Sabarthès, *L'Aude*, p. 263, and Bachrach, "Southern Gaul," p. 356, n. 9.

55. Sampigny (Marne): Sampeginiacum, 1170; Sampiniacum, 1171. Longnon, *La Marne*, p. 254.

56. Sampigny (Meuse): Sampiniacum, ninth century, 973, 1047. Félix Liénard, *Dictionnaire topographique du département de la Meuse* (Paris, 1872), p. 216.

Bibliography

Bibliography

Primary Materials

Actus pontificum Cenomannis in urbe degentium, ed. G. Busson and A. Ledru. *Archive historiques du Maine*, vol. II. Le Mans, 1889.

Ambrose. *Expositio Evangelii Secundum Lucam*, ed. C. Schenkl. *CSEL*, vol. XXXII. Vienna, 1902.

Ammianus Marcellinus. *Res gestae*, ed. C. U. Clark. 2 vols. Berlin, 1910–1915.

Arrian. *Acies contra Alanos: Scripta Minora*, ed. A. G. Ross and G. Wirth. Leipzig, 1968.

_____. *Tactica: Scripta Minora*, ed. A. G. Ross and G. Wirth. Leipzig, 1968.

Aulularia sive Querolus, ed. R. Peiper. Leipzig, 1875. *Griesgram oder die Geschichte vom Topf: Querolus sive Aulularia*, ed. W. Ermich. Berlin, 1965.

Ausonius. *Ephemeris*, ed. C. Schenkl. *MGH AA*, vol. V, pt. 2. Berlin, 1883.

Avienus: Festus Rufus Avienus. *Descriptio Orbis Terrae*, ed. E. Baehrens. *PLM*, vol. V. Paris, 1825.

Bayeux Tapestry, 2nd ed., ed. F. M. Stenton. London, 1965.

Bede. *Chronica*, ed. T. Mommsen. *MGH AA*, vol. XIII. Berlin, 1898.

Bouquet, M. *Recueil des historiens des Gaules et de la France*, vol. III. Paris, 1840–1904.

Candidus Isaurus. *Fragmenta*, ed. C. Muller. *FHG*, vol. IV. Paris, 1868.

Cartulaire de l'Abbaye de Conques, ed. G. Desjardins. Paris, 1879.

Chron. Caesaraug., s.a.: Chronicorum Caesaraugustanorum reliquiae a. CCCCL–DLXVIII, ed. T. Mommsen. *MGH AA*, vol. XI, reprint. Berlin, 1961.

Chron. Gall.: Chronica Gallica a. CCCCLII et DXI, ed. T. Mommsen. *MGH AA*, vol. IX. Berlin, 1892.

Chronicon Monasterri de Bello, ed. J. S. Brewer. London, 1846.

Chronographus anni CCCLIII, ed. T. Mommsen. *MGH AA*, vol. IX. Berlin, 1892.

Claudian. *Carmina*, ed. T. Birt. *MGH AA*, vol. X. Berlin, 1892.

A History of the Alans

Claudius Marius Victor. *Alethia,* ed. C. Schenkl. *CSEL,* vol. XVI. Vienna, 1888.

Cosmog. Rav.: *Ravennatis Anonymi Cosmographer et Guidonis Geographia,* ed. J. Schnetz. *Itineria Romana,* vol. II. Leipzig, 1940.

CTh: Codex Theodosianus, ed. T. Mommsen. Berlin, 1905.

Dio Cassius: *Cassii Dionis Cocceiani Historiarum Romanarum quae supersunt,* ed. I. Bekker. Leipzig, 1849. See also the editions by J. P. Boissevain, Berlin, 1895–1931, and J. Melber, 2 vols., Leipzig, 1890–1928.

Dionysius Perigetes, ed. A. Garzya. Leipzig, 1963.

Dracontius. *Romulea,* ed. F. Vollmer. *MGH AA,* vol. XIV. Berlin, 1905.

Epitome de Caesaribus, ed. F. Pichlmayr. Leipzig, 1911.

Evagrius Scholasticus. *Ecclesiastical History,* trans. Attributed to W. Walford. London, 1846.

Fasti Vindobonenses priores, ed. T. Mommsen. *MGH AA,* vol. IX. Berlin, 1892.

Fortunatus. *In laudem Sanctae Mariae,* ed. F. Leo. *MGH AA,* vol. IV, pt. 1. Berlin, 1881.

Fred.: *Chronicarum quae dicuntur Fredegarii scholastici libri IV,* ed. B. Krusch. *MGH SSRM,* vol. II. Hannover, 1888.

Gaimar, Geffrei. *L'Estoire des Engleis,* ed. A. Bell. Oxford, 1860.

Geoffrey of Monmouth. *Historia Regum Britanniae,* ed. E. Faral. *La légende arthurienne,* vol. III. Paris, 1929.

Gesta Theodorici regis, ed. B. Krusch. *MGH SSRM,* vol. II. Hannover, 1888.

Gregory. *G.M.: Gregorii episcopi Turonensis, Liber in Gloria Martyrum,* ed. B. Krusch. *MGH SSRM,* vol. I. Hannover, 1885.

————. *Hist.: Gregorii episcopi Turonensis, Libri Historiarum,* ed. B. Krusch and W. Levison. *MGH SSRM,* vol. I, pt. 1. Hannover, 1951.

————. *Historia Francorum,* ed. B. Krusch and W. Levison. *MGH SSRM,* vol. I, pt. 1. Hannover, 1937–1951.

HA: Scriptores Historiae Augustae, ed. H. Hohl. Leipzig, 1927.

Hadrian. *Carmina Latina Epigraphica,* ed. F. Bücher, vol. II. Leipzig, 1907. See also *Inscriptiones Christianae Urbis Romae,* ed. D. De Rossi, vol. II. Rome, 1888.

Hegesippus qui dicitur sive Egesippus de bello Iudaico recognitus, ed. C. F. Weber and J. Caesar. Marburg, 1864.

Hermoldus, *Poème sur Louis le Pieux,* ed. E. Faral. Paris, 1964.

Herodian. *Ab excessu divi Marci libri viii,* ed. K. Stavenhagen. Leipzig, 1922.

Hydatius. *Chronica,* ed. T. Mommsen. *MGH AA,* vol. XI. Berlin 1894.

Isidore. *Etymologiae sive Origines,* ed. W. M. Lindsay. 2 vols. Oxford, 1911.

————. *Hist. Goth.: Isidori Iunioris episcopi Hispalensis, historia Gothorum, Wandalorum, Sueborum, ad, a DCXXIV,* ed. T. Mommsen. *MGH AA,* vol. XI, reprint. Berlin, 1961.

Jerome. *Lettres,* ed. and trans. J. Labourt. 8 vols. Paris, 1949–1963.

John of Antioch. *Fragmenta. FHG,* IV (1868), 538–622, V (1870), 27–38.

John Biclar: *Johannis abbatis Biclarensis chronica a DLXVII–DXC,* ed. T. Mommsen. *MGH AA,* vol. XI, reprint. Berlin, 1961.

Jordanes. *Getica: Jordanis, De origine actibus Getarum,* ed. T. Mommsen. *MGH AA,* vol. V, pt. 1, reprint. Berlin, 1961.

————. *Romana,* ed. T. Mommsen. *MGH AA,* vol. V, pt. 1. Berlin, 1882.

Josephus. *Antiquitates Judaicae: Opera Omnia,* ed. S. Naber. 6 vols. Leipzig, 1888–1896.

BIBLIOGRAPHY

_____. *De Bello Judaico: Opera Omnia*, ed. S. Naber. 6 vols. Leipzig, 1888–1896.

Julius Valerius: *Iulii Valerii Res gestae Alexandri*, ed. B. Kübler. Leipzig, 1888.

Justinian. *Novellae*, ed. R. Schoell and W. Kroll. Berlin, 1895.

Legenda sancti Geoznovii, ed. A. De la Borderie, in *L'Historia Britonum et l'Historia Britannica avant Geoffroi de Monmouth*. Paris, 1883.

Lex Salica, 100 Titel-Text, ed. K. A. Eckhardt. Weimar, 1953.

Lex Visigothorum, ed. K. Zeumer. *MGH LL*, vol. I. Hannover and Leipzig, 1902.

L.H.F.: Liber Historiae Francorum, ed. B. Krusch. *MGH SSRM*, vol. II. Hannover, 1888.

Lucan. *De Bello Civili*, ed. C. Hosius. Leipzig, 1913.

Lucian. *Toxaris: Opera*, ed. C. Jacobitz. 3 vols. Leipzig, 1909–1913.

Malalas: John Malalas. *Chronographia*, ed. L. Dindorf. Bonn, 1831.

Marcellinus V. C. Comes. *Chronicon*, ed. T. Mommsen. *MGH AA*, vol. XI. Berlin, 1894.

Martial. *Epigrammata*, ed. W. Gilbert. Leipzig, 1912.

Martin of Braga: *Martini episcopi Bracarensis opera omnia*, ed. C. W. Barlow. New Haven, 1950.

Nennius. *Historia Brittonum*, ed. F. Lot. 2 vols. Paris, 1934.

Nithard. *Histoire des fils de Louis le Pieux*, ed. P. Lauer. Paris, 1964.

Notitia Dignitatum utriusque imperii, ed. O. Seeck. Berlin, 1876.

Notker. *Gesta Karoli Magni Imperatoris*, ed. H. Haefele. *MGH SSRG n.s.* Berlin, 1959.

Olymp.: Olympiodorus of Thebes. *Fragments*, ed. C. Muller. *FHG*, vol. IV. Paris, 1868.

Origo gentis Langobardorum, ed. G. Waitz. *MGH SSRL*, vol. I, Hannover, 1878.

Orosius. *Historiarum adversus paganos libri vii*, ed. C. Zangemeister. Leipzig, 1889.

Pacatus. *Panegyrici Latini*, ed. W. Baehrens. Leipzig, 1911.

Pardessus. *Diplomata, Chartae, Epistulae, Leges . . .* , ed. Jean Marie Pardessus. 2 vols., reprint. Darmstadt, 1969.

Paul. *Hist.: Pauli Diaconi Historia Langobardorum*, ed. L. Bethmann and G. Waitz. *MGH SSRL*, vol. I. Hannover, 1878.

Paulinus of Beziers. *Epigramma*, ed. C. Schenkl. *CSEL*, vol. XVI. Vienna, 1888.

Paulinus of Nola. *Carmina*, ed. W. de Hartel. *CSEL*, vol. XXX. Vienna, 1894.

Paulinus of Pella. *Eucharisticos*, ed. W. Brandes. *CSEL*, vol. XVI. Vienna, 1888.

Philostorgius. *Historia Ecclesiastica*, ed. J. Bidez. Berlin, 1913.

Pliny. *Naturalis Historia*, ed. C. Mayhoff. 5 vols. Leipzig, 1897–1909.

Possidius. *Vita S. Augustini*, ed. H. Weiskotten. Princeton, 1919.

Priscus of Panium. *Fragments*, ed. C. Muller. *FHG*, vol. IV. Paris, 1868.

Procopius. *Opera omnia*, 2nd ed., ed. J. Haury and G. Wirth. 4 vols. Leipzig, 1962–1964.

Prosp. *Epit. Chron.: Prosperi Tironis epitoma Chronicon*, ed. T. Mommsen. *MGH AA*, vol. IX. Berlin, 1892.

Pseudo-Callisthenes. *Historia Alexandri Magni*, ed. W. Kroll. Berlin, 1926.

Ptolemy. *Geographica*, ed. C. Nubbe. Leipzig, 1898.

A HISTORY OF THE ALANS

Regino of Prüm. *Chronicon*, ed. F. Kurze. *MGH SSRG ius*. Hannover, 1890.
Ruodlieb, ed. H. Zeydel. Chapel Hill, 1959.
Saga of King Heidrek the Wise, The, ed. C. Tolkien. London, 1960.
Salvian. *De gubernatione Dei*, ed. C. Halm. *MGH AA*, vol. I, pt. 1. Berlin, 1877.
Seneca. *Thyestes: L. Annaei Senecae Tragoediae*, ed. R. Peiper and G. Richter. Leipzig, 1902.
Sidonius Apollinaris. *Sidonii Apollinaris, Epistulae et Carmina*, ed. C. Luetjohann. *MGH AA*, vol. VIII. Berlin, 1887.
Sozomen. *Historia Ecclesiastica*, ed. J. Bidez and G. C. Hansen. Berlin, 1960.
Suetonius. *Vita duodecim Caesarum*, ed. M. Ihm. Leipzig, 1923.
Tabula Peutingeriana: Die Peutingersche Tafel, ed. K. Miller. Stuttgart, 1962.
Tacitus, *Annales*, ed. E. Koestermann. Leipzig, 1960.
————. *Historiarum Libri*, ed. E. Koestermann. Leipzig, 1960.
Theophanes. *Chronographia*, ed. C. De Boor. 2 vols. Leipzig, 1883–1885.
Thesaurus Linguae Latinae, Onomasticon, vol. II. Leipzig, 1907–1913.
V. Arnulfi, ed. B. Krusch. *MGH SSRM*, vol. II. Hannover, 1888.
V. Cadoci, ed. W. J. Rees. *Lives of Cambro-British Saints*. Landovery, 1853.
V. Carantoci, ed. W. J. Rees. *Lives of Cambro-British Saints*. Landovery, 1853.
V. Dan.: Vita S. Danielis Stylitae, ed. M. Delehaye. *Analecta Bollandiana*, XXXII (1913), 121–214.
V. Germani: episcopi Autissiodorensis autore Constantio, ed. W. Levison. *MGH SSRM*, vol. VII. Hannover and Leipzig, 1920. *Constance de Lyon: Vie de Saint Germain d'Auxerre*, ed. R. Borius. *Sources chrétiennes*, vol. CCXII. Paris, 1965.
V. Gildae, ed. H. Williams. London, 1889.
V. Goaris, ed. B. Krusch. *MGH SSRM*, vol. II. Hannover, 1902.
V. Paterni, ed. W. J. Rees. *Lives of Cambro-British Saints*. Landovery, 1853.
V. Paul: Vita Sancti Pauli, ed. Dom F. Plaine. *Analecta Bollandiana*, I (1882), 208–258.
V. Samson: La Vie de Saint Samson, ed. R. Fawtier. Paris, 1912.
V. Teilo: Life of Saint Teilo, ed. W. J. Rees. *Liber Landavensis*. Landovery, 1840.
Valerius Flaccus. *Argonautica*, ed. O. Kramer. Leipzig, 1913.
Vegetius. *Epitoma rei militaris*, ed. C. Lang. Leipzig, 1885.
Vict. Vit.: Victor Vitensis. *Historia persecutionis Africae*, ed. C. Halm. *MGH AA*, vol. III. Berlin, 1879.
Victor Tonn.: *Victor Tonnennensis episcopi chronica a. CCCCXLIV–DLXVII*, ed. T. Mommsen. *MGH AA*, vol. IX, reprint. Berlin, 1961.
Wace: *Maistre Wace's Roman de Rou et des Ducs de Normandie*, ed. Hugo Andresen. London, 1879.
William of Malmesbury. *De Gestis Regum Anglorum*, ed. W. Stubbs. London, 1889.
William of Poitiers. *Gesta Guillelmi Ducis Normannorum et Regis Anglorum*, ed. R. Foreville. Paris, 1952.
Zonaras. *Epitome historiarum*, ed. L. Dindorf. 6 vols. Leipzig, 1868–1875.
Zosimus. *Historia Nova*, ed. L. Mendelssohn. Leipzig, 1887.

BIBLIOGRAPHY

Secondary Materials

Åberg, Nils. *The Occident and the Orient in the Art of the Seventh Century*, pt. 3. Stockholm, 1947.

Alföldi, A. "Funde aus der Hunnenzeit un ihre ethniche Sonderung," *Archaeologica Hungarica*, IX (Budapest, 1932).

Allen, W. E. D. *David Allens: The History of a Family Firm, 1857–1957*. London, 1957.

Altheim, Franz. *Geschichte der Hunnen*, vols. I, IV. Berlin 1959, 1962.

Anderson, A. "Alexander and the Caspian Gates," *Transactions of the American Philosophical Association*, LIX (1928).

_____. *Alexander's Gate: Gog Magog and the Enclosed Nations*. Cambridge, Mass., 1932.

Anderson, J. G. C. "The Eastern Frontier from Tiberius to Nero," *CAH*, X (1934), 743–780.

Bachrach, Bernard S. "The Alans in Gaul," *Tradito*, XXIII (1967), 476–489.

_____. "A Note on Alites," *Byzantinische Zeitschrift*, LXI (1968), 35.

_____. "Another Look at the Barbarian Settlement in Southern Gaul," *Traditio*, XXV (1969), 354–358.

_____. "The Origin of Armorican Chivalry," *Technology and Culture*, X (1969), 166–171.

_____. "Procopius, Agathias, and the Frankish Military," *Speculum*, XLV (1970), 435–441.

_____. "Procopius and the Chronology of Clovis's Reign," *Viator*, I (1970), 21–31.

_____. "The Feigned Retreat at Hastings," *Mediaeval Studies*, XXXIII (1971), 344–347.

_____. *Review*: S. Rudenko, *The Frozen Tombs of Siberia*. *AHR*, LXXVI (1971), 754.

_____. *Review*: T. Sulimirski, *The Sarmatians*. *AHR*, LXXVI (1971), 1525–1526.

_____. *Merovingian Military Organization, 481–751*. Minneapolis, 1972.

_____. "Two Alan Motifs in Åberg's Aquitanian Style," *Central Asiatic Journal*, XVI (1972), 82–94.

Baedeker, Karl. *Southern France*. 6th ed. Leipzig, 1914.

Bailey, H. W. "Iranian AYRA- and DAHA-," *Transactions of the Philological Society* (1959), pp. 71–115.

Baschmakoff, Alexandre. *La synthèse des périplus pontiques*. Paris, 1948.

Baynes, N. H. "A Note on Professor Bury's 'History of the Later Roman Empire,'" *JRS*, XII (1922), 207–229.

Beeler, John. *Warfare in England, 1066–1189*. Ithaca, N.Y., 1966.

Beninger, Edouard. "Der westgotisch-alanische Zug nach Mitteleuropa," *Mannus Bibliothek*, LI (1931).

Bergengruen, Alexander. *Adel und Grundherrschaft in Merowingerreich*. Weisbaden, 1958.

Bersanetti, G. M. "Basilisco e l'imperatore Leone I," *Rendiconti della Pontifica Accademia di Archeologia*, XX (1943–1944), 331–346.

Blosseville, B. E. de. *Dictionnaire topographique du département de l'Eure*. Paris, 1877.

Bournatzeff, A. "Noms toponymiques des lieux historiques en France," *Oss-Alains*, I (1953), 21–22.

Brooks, E. W. "The Emperor Zenon and the Isaurians," *EHR*, XXX (1893), 209–238.

A HISTORY OF THE ALANS

Brun-Durand, J. *Dictionnaire topographique du département de la Drôme.* Paris, 1891.

Bunbury, E. H. *A History of Ancient Geography.* 2 vols. 2nd ed. London, 1883.

Bury, J. B. "The Notitia Dignitatum," *JRS,* X (1920), 131–154.

──────. *History of the Later Roman Empire.* 2 vols. Dover ed. New York, 1958.

Cabié, Edmond. *Droits et possessions du comte de Toulouse dans l'Albigeois au milieu du XIII⁴ siècle.* Albi, 1900.

──────. "Alos en Albigeois aux Xᵉ et XIᵉ siècles," *Revue historique, scientifique et litteraire du département du Tarn,* XXIII (1926), 122–129.

Cameron, Alan. "Theodosius the Great and the Regency of Stilicho," *Harvard Studies,* LXXIII (1968), 247–280.

──────. *Claudian, Poetry and Propaganda at the Court of Honorius.* Oxford, 1970.

Carré de Busserolle, J-X. *Dictionnaire géographique, historique, et biographique d'Indre-et-Loire.* 6 vols. Tours, 1878–1884.

Chadwick, Nora K. *Early Scotland.* Cambridge, 1949.

──────. "The Colonization of Brittany from Celtic Britain," *Proceedings of the British Academy,* LX (1965), 235–299.

──────. *Early Brittany.* Cardiff, 1969.

Chantre, Ernst. *Recherches anthropologiques dans le Caucase.* 4 vols. Paris, 1885–1887.

Christiansen, Peder G. *The Use of Images by Claudius Claudianus.* The Hague, 1969.

Clemente, Guido. *La Notitia Dignitatum.* Cagliari, 1968.

Clover, Frank M. *Flavius Merobaudes. Transactions of the American Philosophical Society,* LXI (1971).

Cocheris, Hippolyte. *Dictionnaire des anciens noms des communes du département de Seine-et-Oise.* Versailles, 1874.

Corsaro, F. *Querolus. Studio introduttivo e commentario.* Bologna, 1965.

Courcelle, Pierre. *Histoire littéraire des grandes invasions germaniques.* Paris, 1948.

Courtois, Christian. *Les Vandales et l'Afrique.* Paris, 1955.

Dain, Alphonse. "Les stratégistes Byzantins," *Travaux et Mémoires,* II (1967), 317–392.

Dauzat, Albert. *La toponymie française.* Paris, 1939.

──────, and Ch. Rostaing. *Dictionnaire étymologique des noms de lieux en France.* Paris, 1963.

David, Charles W. *Robert Curthose.* Cambridge, Mass., 1920.

Debevoise, N. *A Political History of Parthia.* Chicago, 1938.

Dekkers, E. *Clavis Patrum Latinorum.* 2nd ed. In *Sacris erudiri,* III, no. 1044a. Steenbrugge, 1961.

Delbrueck, R. *Die Consular Diptychen und verwandte Denkmäler.* Berlin and Leipzig, 1929.

Delehaye, Hippolyte. *The Legends of the Saints.* London, 1962.

Demandt, A. "Magister militum," *RE* suppl. XII (1970), cols. 553–790.

Demougeot, E. *De l'unité à la division de l'empire romain, 395–410.* Paris, 1951.

Denus, André Rolland de. *Dictionnaire des appellation ethniques de la France et Colonies.* Paris, 1889.

Deric, Gilles. *Histoire ecclésiastique de Bretagne.* 2 vols. Saint-Brieuc, 1847.

BIBLIOGRAPHY

Devic, C., and J. Vaissete, *Histoire générale de Languedoc* (*HGL*). 15 vols. Toulouse, 1872–1892.

Dictionnaire des communes, France metropolitaine, départements d'Outremer, rattachements et statistiques. 31st ed. Paris, 1968.

Diller, Aubrey. *The Tradition of the Minor Greek Geographers. Monographs of the American Philological Association,* XIV (1952).

Dillon, M., and Nora K. Chadwick. *The Celtic Realms.* London, 1967.

Dingwall, Eric. *Artificial Cranial Deformation.* London, 1931.

Dizionario Enciclopedico dei comuni d'Italia. Rome, 1950.

Eadie, J. W. "The Development of Roman Mailed Cavalry," *JRS,* LVII (1967), 161–173.

Enciclopedia Universal ilustrada. Barcelona, 1907–19– –.

Ewig, Eugen. *Trier im Merowingerreich.* Trier, 1954.

_____. "L'Aquitaine et les Pays Rhénans au haut moyen âge," *Cahiers de civilisation médiévale,* I (1958), 37–54.

Fabre, P. *Essai sur la chronologie de l'oevre de saint Paulin.* Paris, 1948.

Faral, Edmond. *La légende arthurienne.* 3 vols. Paris, 1929.

Ferguson, Alan D., and Alfred Levin, eds. *Essays in Russian History: A Collection Dedicated to George Vernadsky.* Hamden, Conn., 1964.

Fleuriot, J. L. "Recherches sur les enclaves romanes anciennes en territoire brettonant," *Études celtiques,* VIII (1959), 164–178.

Franchet, L. "Une colonie Scytho-Alaine en Orléanais au Vᵉ siècle," *Revue scientifique,* LXVIII (1930), 70–82, 109–117.

Frank, Richard. *Scholae Palatinae.* Rome, 1969.

Galeron, F. *Statistique de l'arrondissement de Falaise.* Falaise, 1828.

Ganshof, F. L. "Note sur le sens de 'Ligeris' au titre XLVII de la loi salique et dans le 'Querolus.'" In *Historical Essays in Honour of James Tait,* pp. 111–120. Manchester, 1933.

Gautier, E. F. *Genséric Roi des Vandales.* Paris, 1935.

Giordani, G. *La colonia tedesca di Alagna-Valsesia e il suo dialetto.* Torino, 1881.

Goffart, Walter. *The Le Mans Forgeries: A Chapter from the History of Church Property in the 9th Century.* Cambridge, Mass., 1966.

Grande Encyclopédie, La. 31 vols. Paris, 1886–1902.

Gregoire, Henri. "Où en est la question des Nibelungen?" *Byzantion,* X (1935), 215–245.

Grenier, A. *Manuel d'archéologie Gallo-romaine,* vols. V, VI. Paris, 1931, 1934.

Gröhler, H. *Ueber Ursprung und Bedeutung der französischen Ortsnamen.* 2 vols. Heidelberg, 1913–1935.

Hampel, Joseph. *Alterthümer des frühen Mittelalters in Ungarn.* 3 vols. Brunswick, 1905.

Hanning, Robert. *The Vision of History in Early Britain.* New York, 1966.

Havet, L. *Le Querolus.* Paris, 1880.

Herrmann, P. "Massagetai," *RE,* cols. 2124–2129.

Hippeau, C. *Dictionnaire topographique du département du Calvados.* Paris, 1883.

Hodgkin, Thomas. *Italy and Her Invaders.* 8 vols. Oxford, 1885–1889.

Hollister, Warren. *Anglo-Saxon Military Institutions.* Oxford, 1962.

Jackson, Kenneth. *Language and History in Early Britain.* Cambridge, Mass., 1953.

Jacot, Arthur. *Schweizerisches Ortslexikon.* Lucerne, 1969.

A HISTORY OF THE ALANS

Jesse, George R. *Researches into the History of the British Dog.* 2 vols. London, 1886.

Jolibois, Emile. "Aquelle epoque vivait St. Alain?" *Revue historique, scientifique et litteraire du département du Tarn,* I (1877), 141–142, 154–155, 183–186.

Jones, A. H. M. *The Later Roman Empire.* 2 vols. Norman, Okla., 1964.

Junghans, W. "Histoire Critique des règnes de Childeric et de Chlodovech." Trans. and augmented by G. Monod. *BEHE,* XXXVII (1879).

Justi, Ferdinand. *Iranisches Namenbuch.* Marburg, 1895.

Kaegi, E. *Byzantium and the Decline of Rome.* Princeton, 1968.

Kruglikova, I. T. *Bospor v pozdneantichnoe vremia.* Moscow, 1966.

Kulakovsky, Iu. *Alany po svedeniiam klassicheskikh i vizantiiskikh pisatelei.* Kiev, 1899.

Kurth, G. *Histoire poétique des Mérovingiens.* Brussels and Leipzig, 1893.

Kusnetzov, V. A. "Alanskie Plemena Severnogo Kaukaza," *Materialy i issledovaniia po Arkheologii SSSR,* CVI (Moscow, 1962).

————, and V. K. Pudovin. "Alany v Zapadnoi Europe v epokhu 'Velikogo pereseleniia narodov,'" *Sovetskaia Arkheologiia,* II (1961), 79–85.

Lacger, Louis de. *États administratifs des anciens diocèses d'Albi, de Castres, et de Lavaur.* Albi, 1929.

Lair, L. "Conjectures sur les chapitres XVIII et XIX du livre II de l'*Historia Ecclesiastica* de Grégoire de Tours," *Annuaire-Bulletin de la Société de l'Histoire de France,* XXXV (1898), 3–29.

Lepage, Henri. *Dictionnaire topographique du département de la Muerthe.* Paris, 1862.

Levison, W. "Bischof Germanus von Auxerre und die Quellen zu seiner Geschichte," *Neues Archiv der Gesellschaft für ältere deutsche Geschichtskunde,* XXIX (1903), 95–175.

Leyser, Karl. "The Battle of Lech," *History,* L (1965), 1–25.

————. "Henry I and the Beginnings of the Saxon Empire," *EHR,* LXXXIII (1968), 1–32.

Liénard, Félix. *Dictionnaire topographique du département de la Meuse.* Paris, 1872.

Lobineau, Guy. *Histoire de Bretagne.* 2 vols. Paris, 1707.

————. *Les vies de Saints de Bretagne.* 5 vols. Paris, 1836–1837; new ed., 1886.

Longnon, Auguste. *Géographie de la Gaule au VIᵉ siècle.* Paris, 1878.

————. *Dictionnaire topographique du département de la Marne.* Paris, 1891.

————. *Les noms de lieux de la France.* Paris, 1920.

Loomis, C. Grant. "King Arthur and the Saints," *Speculum,* VIII (1933), 478–482.

Loomis, R. S., ed. *Arthurian Literature in the Middle Ages.* Oxford, 1959.

Lot, F. "Les migrations saxonnes en Gaule et en Grande-Bretagne," *RH,* CXIX (1915), 1–40.

————. "Du régime de hospitalité," *RBPH,* VII (1928), 975–1011.

————. "La conquête du pays d'entre Seine-et-Loire par les Francs," *RH,* CLXIV (1930), 241–253.

————. *Nennius et l'Historia Brittonum.* 2 vols. Paris, 1934.

Loth, Joseph. "La vie de Saint Teliau," *Annales de Bretagne,* IX (1893), 80–95.

————. *Les noms des Saints Bretons.* Paris, 1910.

BIBLIOGRAPHY

Loyen, André, "Le rôle de Saint Aignan dans la défense d'Orléans," *Comptes Rendus: Académie des Inscriptions et Belles-Lettres* (Paris, 1969), pp. 64–74.

Maenchen-Helfen, Otto. "Huns and Hsiung-Nu," *Byzantion*, XVII (1944–1945), 222–243.

Martonne, A. de. "Deux nouveaux évêques du Mans," *Revue historique de l'ouest*, I (1885), 506–515.

Matton, Auguste. *Dictionnaire topographique du département de l'Aisne.* Paris, 1871.

Mazzarino, S. *Stilicone: La crisi imperiale dopo Toedosio.* Rome, 1942.

Merlet, Lucien. *Dictionnaire topographique du département d'Eure-et-Loir.* Paris, 1861.

Meyer, W. "Zwei antike Elfenbeintafel der königlisch Staats-Bibliothek in München," *Abhandlungen der Königlisch-Bayerischen Akademie der Wissenschaften*, XV (1879), 1–84.

Minns, Ellis H. *Scythians and Greeks.* Cambridge, 1913.

Mócsy, A. "Der Name Flavius als Rangbezeichnung in der Spätantike," *Akte IV Kongress für griechische und lateinische Epigraphik* (Vienna, 1964), pp. 257–263.

Mommsen, T. *Römische Geschichte*, vol. V. Berlin, 1933.

Moreau, Edouard de. *Saint Amand.* Louvain, 1927.

Morice, P. H. *Histoire ecclésiastique et civile de Bretagne.* 20 vols., rev. ed. Guincamp, 1835–1837.

Morlet, Marie-Therese. *Toponymie de la Thierache.* Paris, 1967.

Müllenhoff, Karl. *Deutsche Altertumskunde.* 5 vols. Berlin, 1887–1906.

Nègre, E. *Les noms de lieux du Tarn.* 2nd ed. Paris, 1957.

Olivieri, Dante. *Dizionario di Toponomastica Lombarda.* 2nd ed. Milan, 1961.

Oman, Charles. *A History of the Art of War in the Middle Ages.* 2 vols. London, 1924.

Oost, S. I. *Galla Placidia Augusta.* Chicago, 1968.

O'Rahilly, Thomas F. *Early Irish History and Mythology.* Dublin, 1946.

Ozols, J. "Alanen," *Reallexikon der germanischen Altertumskunde*, I, pt. 2 (Berlin, 1970), 124–126.

Peisker, T. "The Asiatic Background," *CMH*, I (1911), 331–339.

Perkins, Ward. "The Sculpture of Visigothic France," *Archaeologia*, LXXXVII (1938), 79–128.

Philipon, Edouard. *Dictionnaire topographique du département de l'Ain.* Paris, 1911.

Polaschek, E. "Wiener Grabfunde aus der Zeit des untergehenden römischen Limes," *Wiener Prähistorisch Zeitschrift*, XIX (1932), 239–258.

Quilgars, H. *Dictionnaire topographique du département de la Loire-Inférieure.* Nantes, 1906.

Rawlinson, George. *The Sixth Great Oriental Monarchy.* New York, 1872.

Rees, Rice. *An Essay on the Welsh Saints.* London, 1836.

Reynolds, Robert. "Reconsideration of the History of the Suevi," *RBPH*, XXXV (1957), 19–47.

———, and Robert Lopez. "Odoacer: German or Hun?" *AHR*, LII (1946), 36–53.

Rosenzweig, M. *Dictionnaire topographique du département du Morbihan.* Paris, 1870.

Roserot, A. *Dictionnaire topographique du département de la Haute-Marne.* Paris, 1903.

151

A History of the Alans

Rostovtzeff, M. I. *Iranians and Greeks in South Russia*. Oxford, 1922.
————. "La centre de l'Asie, la Russie, la Chine, et le style animal," *Skythika*, I (Prague, 1929).
————. *Skythien und der Bosporus*. Berlin, 1931.
————. "The Sarmatae and the Parthians," *CAH*, XI (1936), 91–130.
Sabarthès, A. *Dictionnaire topographique du département de l'Aude*. Paris, 1912.
Sandbach, F. H. "Greek Literature, Philosophy, and Science," *CAH*, XI (1963), 676–707.
Sanford, E. M. "Nero and the East," *Harvard Studies in Classical Philology*, XLVIII (1937), 75–103.
Sawyer, P. H. *The Age of the Vikings*. London, 1962.
Schmidt, Ludwig. *Geschichte der deutschen Stämme*. 2 vols. in 3 pts. Berlin, 1910, 1911, 1918.
————. *Geschichte der Wandalen*. Munich, 1942.
Schwartz, E. "Arrianus," *RE*, II, cols. 1230–1247.
Slicher van Bath, B. H. "Dutch Tribal Problems," *Speculum*, XXIX (1949), 319–338.
Smith, D. H. *Chinese Religions*. London, 1968.
Stadter, P. "Flavius Arrianus: The New Xenophon," *Greek, Roman, and Byzantine Studies*, VIII (1967), 155–161.
Stein, Ernst. *Histoire du bas-empire*. 2 vols. Paris, 1949–1959.
Stroheker, K. F. "Studien zu den historisch-geographischen Grundlagen der Nibelungendichtung," *Deutsche Vierteljahrschrift für Literaturwissenschaft und Geistesgeschichte*, XXXII (1958), 216–240. Reprinted in *Germanentum und Spätantike*. Stuttgart, 1965.
————. *Germanentum und Spätantike*. Stuttgart, 1965.
Sulimirski, T. *The Sarmatians*. New York, 1970.
Syme, Ronald. "Falvian Wars and Frontiers," *CAH*, IX (1963), 131–187.
————. *Ammianus and the Historia Augusta*. Oxford, 1968.
————. *Emperors and Biography*. Oxford, 1971.
Täckholm, Ulf. "Aetius and the Battle on the Catalunian Plains," *Opuscula Romana*, VII (1969), 259–276.
Tatlock, J. S. P. "The Dates of the Arthurian Saints' Legends," *Speculum*, XIV (1939), 345–365.
————. *The Legendary History of Britain*. Berkeley, 1950.
Täubler, E. *Die Parthernachrichten bei Josephus*. Berlin, 1904.
————. "Zur Geschichte der Alanen," *Klio*, IX (1909), 14–28.
Thompson, E. A. "The Isaurians under Theodosius II," *Hermathena*, LXVIII (1946), 18–31.
————. *The Historical Work of Ammianus Marcellinus*. Cambridge, 1947.
————. *A History of Attila and the Huns*. Oxford, 1948.
————. "The Foreign Policies of Theodosius II and Marcian," *Hermathena*, LXXV (1950), 58–75.
————. "The Settlement of the Barbarians in Southern Gaul," *JRS*, XLVI (1956), 65–75.
————. "A Chronological Note on St. Germanus of Auxerre," *Analecta Bollandiana*, LXXV (1957), 135–138.
————. "The Visigoths from Fritigern to Euric," *Historia*, XV (1963), 105–126.
————. *The Early Germans*. Oxford, 1965.
————. *The Visigoths in the Time of Ulfila*. Oxford, 1966.
————. *The Goths in Spain*. Oxford, 1969.

BIBLIOGRAPHY

Tomaschek, W. "Alanen," *RE*, I, cols. 1282–1285.

———. "Albanoi," *RE*, I, cols. 1305–1307.

———. "Borani," *RE*, I, col. 719.

———. "Buri," *RE*, I, col. 1067.

Uhden, R. "Bemerkungen zu dem römischen Kartenfragment von Dura Europos," *Hermes*, LXVII (1932), 117–125.

Vasiliev, A. A. *The Goths in Crimea*. Cambridge, Mass., 1936.

Vernadsky, George. "Goten und Anten in Südrussland," *Südostdeutsche Forschungen*, III (1938), 265–279.

———. "On the Origins of the Antae," *Journal of the American Oriental Society*, LIX (1939), 56–66.

———. "Flavius Ardabur Aspar," *Südostdeutsche Forschungen*, VI (1941), 38–73.

———. *Ancient Russia*. New Haven, 1943.

———. "Sur l'origine des Alains," *Byzantion*, XVI (1943), 81–86.

———. "The Eurasian Nomads and Their Art in the History of Civilization," *Saeculum*, I (1950), 74–85.

———. "Der sarmatisch Hintergrund der germanischen Völkerwanderung," *Saeculum*, II (1951), 340–392.

———. "Anent the Epic Poetry of the Alans," *Mélanges Henri Grégoire (Annuaire de l'Institut de Philologie et d'Histoire Orientales et Slaves)*, XII (1952), 517–538.

———. *The Origins of Russia*. Oxford, 1959.

———. "Eurasian Nomads and Their Impact on Medieval Europe," *Studi Medievali*, 3rd ser., IV (1963), 401–434.

Vinaver, Eugene. "King Arthur's Sword," *Bulletin of the John Rylands Library*, XL (1958), 513–526.

Wagner, Norbert. *Getica*. Berlin, 1967.

Wainwright, F. T. *Archaeology and Place-Names and History*. London, 1962.

Wallace-Hadrill, J. M. *Review:* A Bergengruen, *Adel und Grundherrschaft in Merowingerreich*. *EHR*, LXXV (1960), 483–485.

———. *The Long-Haired Kings*. London, 1962.

Walther, Hans. "Namenkunde und Archäologie im Dienste frühgeschichtlicher Forschung," *Probleme des frühen Mittelalters in archäologischer und historischer Sicht* (Berlin, 1966), pp. 155–168.

Wenskus, R. "Alanen," *Reallexikon der germanischen Altertumskunde*, I, pt. 2 (Berlin, 1970), 122–124.

Werner, Joachim. *Beiträge zur Archäologie des Attila-Reiches*. Munich, 1956.

Wilhelm, R. *The I Ching*. London, 1951.

Index

Index

Pollentia, 34, 38; Tinchebrai, 80, 90; Verona, 35, 38
Bayeux Tapestry, 91
Bede, 75, 114
Belisarius, 57
Beogar, King, 33
Beowulf, 110
Bosphorians, 110
Bourg Théroulde, 90
Brémule, 90
Bretons, 86–92
Britons, 81, 83, 86
Brutus, 83
Burgundians, 60, 62, 69, 78, 81, 82, 100, 101
Buri, 13

Cad- element, 108
Caduon, 108
Caesar, 4, 9, 46
Caladbolg, 110
Caledvwch, 110
Calibs, 110
Caliburn, 110
Callisthenes, pseudo-, 16
Candac, King, 50
Canis Alani, 119
Cappadocians, 7
Carolingians, 84, 87
Carthage, 43
Celts, 84, 85, 105, 107, 108, 113, 136
Chaldeans, 16
Châlons, 77
Charlemagne, 110
Chersonesus, 44
Childebert I, King, 84, 94
Childeric I, King, 77, 78, 84
Childeric III, King, 104
Chintasuintus, King Flavius, 102
Cilicians, 7
Claudian, 35, 76
Clovis, 75, 78, 84, 85
Coloni, 117
Comites Alani, 36
Commodus, Emperor, 13
Conomor, Mark, 80, 84, 108, 114
Conon Meriadoc, 112
Constantine I, Emperor, 37
Constantine III, Emperor, 54, 55, 60
Constantius, author, 115
Constantius, military commander, 29, 30, 56, 57

Dacians, 6, 7
Dagobert I, King, 104
Dapates, 16
Daphnus the Corinthian, 127
Daucones, 16
Deda, 103
Deiotarus, King of Galatia, 4
Demetrius, 127
Dio Cassius, 10
Diocletian, Emperor, 16, 17
Dionysius Periegetes, 10–12, 16
Domitian, Emperor, 6
Dracontius, 57
Durendal, 110

Egyptians, 7
English, 91–92
Eochar, Eocharich, 96, 97, 115. *See also* Goar
Ermanrich, King, 26
Eugenius, 41
Euonyitae, 16
Euthar, Eutharic, 97, 98, 117. *See also* Goar
Evagrius, 45
Excalibur, 110

Fortunatus, 75
Francio, 82
Franks, 15, 52–54, 59, 77, 78, 81–84, 94, 100, 101
Fredbal, King, 56
Fredegar, 82–84
Frederic, Prince, 77
Friga (Frigii, Frigiiae), 82, 83
Fritigern, King, 27, 28

Gainas, 41
Gaiseric, King, 42–47
Galla Placidia, 64
Gallo-Romans, 54, 63–65, 77, 93–94
Geloni, 11, 18
Geoffrey of Monmouth, 86, 87, 109, 110, 112, 113
Geraspus, Flavius (Gerasp), 102, 103
Germans, 6, 7, 15, 21, 41, 42, 49, 50, 58, 72, 76, 97
Germanus, Bishop, *see* St. Germanus
Gerontius, 54, 55
Gesalic, King, 94
Getae, 6, 11
Goar, 53, 59, 60, 62–65, 69, 74, 76, 77, 97, 98, 115. *See also* Eochar,

INDEX

Verus, 128
Vespasian, Emperor, 6, 8
Victor, Claudius Marius, 31–32
Vidiani, 18
Visigoths, 27–29, 31, 56, 57, 61, 65–67, 71, 74, 76–79, 85, 91, 93, 94, 97, 98, 100, 101. *See also* Goths, Germans
Vithimiris, 26
Vologasus I, King, 6

Vologasus II, King, 10
Vusaces, 129

William of Malmesbury, 92
William of Poitiers, 92

Xenophon, *see* Arrianus

Zalboi, 16
Zeno, Emperor, 46, 48

DATE DUE